PANTA REIKI
Soul Healing through Reiki

Panta Rhei

The name of this book is inspired by the ancient Greek philosopher, Heraclitus, who lived in the 6th Century BC.

*Heraclitus is credited with the phrase '****panta rhei****', which means 'everything flows'. Also spelled as **pantarei**, it refers to the concept of impermanence and constant change being at the heart of our existence. Along this same theme, Heraclitus also said, "no man ever steps in the same river twice for it's not the same river and he is not the same man."*

The same philosophy is called anicca in Buddhism, which is an embracing of impermanence because everything that rises then passes. It is the same philosophy behind phrases such as 'this too will pass', 'the only constant is change', and 'go with the flow'.

This state of impermanence is why we are encouraged to not get attached to things, situations or conditions, as it is inevitable that they will all change in time. To be too attached and therefore to resist this change is to invite our own suffering.

I felt this philosophy of 'everything flows' was a wonderful one to marry with the system of Reiki, which is the flow of spiritual energy to bring about change in the way of healing a person's mind, body and soul.

And so this book, Panta Reiki was born.

PANTA REIKI
Soul Healing through Reiki

Copyright © 2020 Gaetano Vivo

This edition published by Gaetano Vivo in 2023
First published in 2020

Graphics and art by Mario Compostella
www.mariocompostella.com

The rights of Gaetano Vivo to be identified as the author of this work have been asserted in accordance with sections 77 and 78 of the Copyright, Designs and Patents Act 1988.
All rights reserved. No part of this work may be reproduced in any material form (including photocopying or storing in any medium by electronic means and whether or not transiently or incidentally to some other use of this publication) without the written permission of the copyright holder except in accordance with the provisions of the Copyright, Designs and Patents Act 1988. Applications for the copyright holder's written permission to reproduce any part of this publication should be addressed to Gaetano Vivo via his website: www.gaetanovivo.com.

ISBN: 978-1-915351-16-6

Gaetano Vivo is
an imprint of
DolmanScott

CONTENTS

Preface	*vii*
Prologue	*ix*
Introduction	*xi*
Chapter 1: *The boy who spoke to angels*	*1*

Part one – The Divine Gift
Chapter 2: *Roots of reiki*	*13*
Chapter 3: *The Masters lineage*	*19*
Chapter 4: *Usui's legacy*	*23*
Chapter 5: *Five principles of Reiki*	*31*

Part two – Heal with Energy
Chapter 6: *Reiki as spiritual energy*	*37*
Chapter 7: *How Reiki works*	*43*
Chapter 8: *Holographic universe*	*47*
Chapter 9: *Reiki is service*	*51*
Chapter 10: *Three levels of Reiki*	*59*
Chapter 11: *The symbols of Reiki*	*71*
Chapter 12: *The teaching of Reiki*	*85*

Part three – Holistic Health
Chapter 13: *Reiki heals your heart*	*93*
Chapter 14: *Dance of the chakras*	*101*
Chapter 15: *Seven major chakras*	*111*
Chapter 16: *Reiki heals your body*	*125*
Chapter 17: *Reiki and oncology*	*129*
Chapter 18: *Reiki heals your mind*	*139*

Part four – The Healing Channel
Chapter 19: *The Vivo Method*	*143*
Chapter 20: *Giving Reiki*	*175*
Chapter 21: *Reiki for animals*	*217*
About the Author	*225*

PREFACE

We live in a time of connection, where the space between things and people disappears.

Space and time – two important elements of existence – reveal themselves to the world here and now, changing the meaning that we seek in everything.

Gaetano Vivo is a man who never stops searching on a journey that brings him closer to worlds, sometimes far, sometimes near, from old wisdoms to new awareness. The path on his spiritual quest leads him to deep knowledge where every tool, every practice, every word, every experience, and every theory is annulled, and sublimated in the ONE. In that place, which is not a place. In that time, which is not a time, where we can perceive the cosmic symmetry between spirit and matter, between the universe and the infinitesimal.

Panta Reiki : The energy of every being - including those we think of as 'inanimate' – flows in a synchronous and circular way, closely related to what we call real.

In this enormous network of endless links, there is a heightened perception of being, at the same time, too small and seemingly useless and so big as to be able to influence everything. It is the power of awareness that wins over duality and makes us better people. The understanding that we call healing, the detachment that sets us free, that 'conversion' that turns every moment of the present into eternity and ourselves into the tools of a HIGHER will, of ANOTHER will capable of smiling at the ego's illusions.

Francesco Italia
Mayor of Syracuse, Sicily

PROLOGUE

Teaching Reiki is above all a responsibility.

I became a Reiki Master in Sedona, a town in the Arizona desert. The red colour of the mountains surrounding that area has given me an energy and inspiration that few other places in the world have given me.

I knew that something really important to me and my life would happen in Sedona. So it was! I met my teacher for the first time in June 1995, during my first stay in that city.

Becoming a Reiki Master was a beautiful experience that transformed and enriched my life. I was looking for something that could make sense of my existence and this was it.

With Reiki, you are able to help people and also be able to alleviate the suffering of others with a simple caress or with a Reiki session. This is something wonderful. I am of the opinion, in fact, that a Reiki practitioner must be someone who is first able to transform themselves before they start to think about transmitting the wisdom of ancient traditions to others.

Reiki is my passion. It has given me the opportunity to reach parallel worlds and it allows us all to go further; to go where the human eye and its elementary perceptions cannot go.

Reiki is an ancient Japanese healing discipline that was rediscovered at the beginning of the 20th century to offer humanity an instrument of change. We have reason to believe that Jesus used Reiki to perform his healing miracles.

The world, in this current era, is undergoing major transformation from an energy point of view and as a result a rapidly growing number of people want to learn natural healing techniques.

We are part of a reality that seems to be evolving in an extraordinary way.

That's why, going forward, Reiki, together with other alternative and complementary healing methods such as sound, crystals, colours and aromas, will be able to take us to a higher level of our super-consciousness.

INTRODUCTION

Today's world needs Reiki.
There are many reasons for this but the main reason is because the principles of holism coexist in Reiki. Holism – which comes from the Greek word όλος meaning 'whole' – is the idea that various systems need to be viewed as wholes; not merely as a collection of parts, because all the parts are so intimately interconnected that they cannot exist independently of the whole. For humans, this means considering the totality of our physical, metaphysical and intellectual parts.
This theory is at the heart of Reiki, which is a gentle, safe and non-intrusive hands-on-healing technique that emerged from Japan in the 1900s. Reiki is a holistic system that sees human beings and their material and spiritual lives as a loop that leads to the Light. More and more people today are waking up to the knowing that the physical dimension is closely connected to the emotional and spiritual dimensions.
Pronounced 'Ray-Kee' in the West, this powerful technique brings back into balance and harmony all the parts that make up human beings – body, mind, emotions, and spirit. This is achieved by using our innate feeling, or frequency, which is Love. People can heal their bodies, minds and spirits thanks to this immense gift.
Before I go any further, it would be helpful to clarify what I mean when I use the term 'healing' and in order to do that, the concept of 'illness' and 'disease' should also be defined.

In English, the term 'disease' has a more objective meaning and describes a pathology, whereas 'illness' has a more subjective nuance, meaning an indisposition or 'feeling' unwell.
In the case of a 'disease', the aim is a solely biological healing based on medicine and surgery whereas, according to the holistic view, 'illness' is nothing but an energy imbalance.
Illness is caused by the negative feelings we all experience every day. Fears, grudges and anger become embedded in our heart, creating an actual biochemical imbalance in our bodies. Often, we realise that generalised stress is the cause of indisposition. In this case, the physical manifestation of stress is a call out from our physical body, which is seeking help for our emotional body. We can therefore see how our bodies and our hearts are interconnected and that's when Reiki can help, by connecting our Spirit to this chain.
Originating from Japan and consisting of a range of energy activations, Reiki takes a holistic view of people to restore their body/mind/spirit balance. Energy is channelled by and through the therapist, who creates a loop between the universe and the client. This facilitates the healing of the spirit and of the heart, which also helps healing the body. This process was frowned upon until recently but has now been accepted by many members of the scientific community. Hospitals and nursing homes all over the world now welcome the use of Reiki as an addition to traditional treatments.
Interest in Reiki has risen exponentially since the 1980s and there are now many millions of practitioners all over the world. Of course, this greater interest has led to interpretation issues and to an excessive superficiality when learning the levels, especially for Level Three, which is when you become a Master.
Reiki practitioners are channels, or conduits, for transmitting energy to those who need it. Channelling Universal Energy is one of the most

wonderful gifts one can receive and share with others. It is an immense gift to give to others and to oneself, because Energy is Love. Therefore, a great sense of responsibility is essential.

No one method is better than any other for practicing Reiki: it is, however, important to approach people in a humble and responsible way, because when they ask for help it means they are weaker. This is why Reiki therapists must see their practice as a 'blessing mission'.

The Reiki method I use is called 'Usui Shiki Ryoho'. It consists of three levels and it follows the lineage of Mikao Usui, Chujiro Hayashi and Hawayo Takata.

In Level One, students are taught what Reiki is and its history, from its discovery by Dr. Mikao Usui at the beginning of the 20th Century, onwards. The course then covers the lineage of the Masters since the origins of Reiki, in recognition of how this discipline has been spread and taught through word of mouth. As well, chakras and their balance are explained, together with self-treatment. Four attunements are given.

Level Two is based on teaching the first three sacred symbols of Reiki; their names and meaning, as well as how to trace or draw them. Distant healing is also taught at this level and an attunement is given. In this book, I will be disclosing the three symbols of this level because there is no reason to keep them secret and, most of all, because they won't work anyway if one is not attuned to Reiki.

Level Three training lasts at least three years. During this time, the conscious student chooses to learn attunement and teaching techniques. At least three years practice are necessary. I do not think that rushing to reach Level Three and becoming a teacher as soon as possible is the best option for someone who is choosing Reiki as their life journey.

No particular qualities are needed to become a Reiki practitioner. Everyone can do it. Reiki therapists are merely energy channels, and people who want to try a Reiki treatment are already prone to healing. Universal Energy knows what to heal.

Reiki therapists can perform many treatments a day because every time they channel energy for a person, they are purified by Universal Energy. Therefore, they do not get tired.

While treating a person, Reiki practitioners experience an increase in their Ki, or life force energy (known as 'ki' in Japan, 'chi' in China and 'prana' in India). They often feel energised, so they can treat several people in succession without feeling weary. The therapist's energy is never weakened because Reiki energy is channelled so that the therapist, too, is purified during a treatment.

Receiving Reiki energy is a unique experience that varies from one treatment to another. Many people describe it as a very relaxing and soothing experience. It aids mental and physical wellbeing and strengthens the immune system. It can relieve physical pain and the symptoms of common colds. Reiki helps overcome sleeplessness, lack of confidence and anxiety. There are no rules in this profession, only ethical and care guidelines.

Having been a Reiki Master for many years, I've taught this beautiful technique to many hundreds of people. I'm including some testimonials from former students here:

"Meeting Reiki Master Gaetano Vivo has been extremely important for me. He is a wonderful and enlightened person, a truly helpful guide who leads you along the path of Light. I met the Master one evening in February last year, at a Reiki event in the home of a very good friend of mine. Many people were attending, and the Master had a kind word for each of us, he explained how our energy body works in connection with our physical body through energy 'wheels' called chakras, through their colours, their spinning movements, their flowing (more or less smoothly) in our physicality and in other parts of us. I

immediately found his words fascinating and intriguing. I related to what he was saying and felt 'at home'. His words were on my wavelength and in step with everything I had perceived about life in terms of subtle energies. That's when I decided I wanted to study this discipline and I completed Levels One and Two of Reiki after attending his classes. Now, I am about to start my journey towards Level Three, hoping I, too, will be able to bring this beautiful small flame of light and wellbeing to every living creature and to everything... Reiki has made my life better, I am filled with love and am immensely grateful for all my life experiences – including the most painful ones – that brought me here and enabled me to share this personal experience with equally wonderful people who have become my soulmates in this extraordinary journey."

Reiki Masters pass on to others the message of love, energy and universal beauty that they have received. Their task is to teach other people how to channel this energy and how to use it to heal themselves and others.
By doing this, they enable each person to look inside themselves and open the doors of their being to let energies flow.
Reiki Masters play a maieutic role because through the attunements and the teachings of the three levels, they deepen every student's self-consciousness and awareness of their role in the world.

Another of my students describes it as follows:

"Reiki is love. Open Reiki is the vehicle through which this message is conveyed. Master Gaetano tells us how universal energies can be channelled through our hands with loving devotion. We are tools; we are channels. We sit on our mats in a circle and we tell each other stories. Disciples, guests, men and women on a quest. Gaetano guides

us with confidence and clarity, enlightened by less and less invisible angels.

"These words unveil the tenderness of a man and a master who welcomes before teaching, and who humbly approaches his students creating a small community where others can blossom so that they can 'feel' the Universe.

"I came across Reiki and Gaetano by coincidence. Or at least that's what I thought in the beginning... Half way through the journey, I realised that what I called minor 'coincidences' were in fact signs deliberately scattered along my path so that, by following them, I could be taken where I was supposed to go."

This is how another student describes her introduction to Reiki:

"I still remember that evening. I was caught up in the frenzy of my hectic work. I felt drained. I had nearly resigned myself to the idea that I was bound to always live like that. I felt helpless, I had lost the meaning of my life and my ambitions, I was leveled out because I constantly had to adapt to everything without being able to react any more. Everything changed that evening. I changed. I cleared my mind. I started seeing things from another perspective, having realised that I could be the enabler of change by learning to accept what I cannot change and by putting myself at the centre of my life. Gaetano Vivo has been the main trigger of this process. A true master and a great guide whom I can never thank enough for giving me back myself.

"Each of us is on a life journey, a pilgrimage that starts with the majestic fragility of being a child.

We carry that child inside ourselves throughout our life. The child lives inside of us and is vulnerable but it is also powerful because it can achieve great things from being close to the whisper of the Universe. This is the child we must reach because it gives us the strength to *channel the energy of Reiki. Our inner child is hidden behind our fears and negative feelings, which are the burdens weighing us down and making us ill. By reaching our inner child, we can release the weight of our daily life and rise.*

Of course, the path is tiring and we may often stumble or even go backwards but it is our inner strength that can help us to take our own hand again.

Today's society expects us to be productive and hyperactive, diverting us from our spiritual search and mindfulness, for which we need time and peacefulness. This is why sometimes we wander off the path that Reiki has laid out in front of us."

.

CHAPTER ONE

THE BOY WHO SPOKE TO ANGELS

I was a very introverted and shy child. I always felt out of place, both with my family and with strangers.

I received a very strict education from my parents. My father especially, was for me a reason for constant quarrels also because of my introversion and shyness. My mother was a special woman. I loved her like I never loved anyone. Growing up, I learned about pure love, love beyond, love that does not ask questions, love of the soul.

My mother was always the sweet and kind person who protected me and spurred me on to be happy in my life. I owe to her what I have become as a human being and, still today, she continues to be a constant source of inspiration for me. She inspires me to help others who are in difficulty. She was like this, she was a listener, always ready to give advice to me or to anyone else who looked to her for help and guidance. Now that she lives in infinity, she has become my guide, my light.

I still miss her terribly today. I miss talking to her, laughing with her, feeling her smile on me. But when I meet her in the afterlife, I realise that I have always had her by my side.

SECRETS AND LIES

Despite his temperament, my father was a respectable, self-made man. He had studied to become a pharmacist, like my grandfather Gaetano, and he became a personality in the country of the Campania province where I grew up.

In Italy, in the early 1960s, there were three important figures in the country: the priest, the doctor and the pharmacist.

He was a strict and very authoritarian father, very concerned about what others thought of him and his family. I can only imagine what it was like for him to have a child who was so different from other teenagers.

He was all work and hunting; I never spent nice carefree days with my father. He was a fan of hunting, and he would sometimes drag me along with him to be amongst the company of men. I hated it. I couldn't bear the thought of killing so many animals.

Occasionally he would bring home an injured bird, which I would take care of and then, once healed, I would release them back to the wild.

Some of my father's friends also participated in these hunting trips. One day, while I was with one of them in the car in one of the moments of rest, I was molested.

I was only nine years old.

That memory has tormented my childhood for a long time, forever marking my life and effectively catapulting me into an early adolescence. All of a sudden, forced, incomprehensible. The world out there no longer made sense to me. I had to protect myself, close myself even more in myself and take refuge in that place of peace and beauty that I kept only for me, the world beyond, populated by angels and invisible beings.

My relationship with my father got worse every day: I remember him calling me "the iceberg" because I kept away from him and I didn't want to hug him or kiss him.

I have always felt unwanted and not appreciated, and for this reason I grew up distancing myself from him until I almost wanted to forget that I had a father.

I was increasingly shy and introverted. I grew up alone, feeling unwanted and unhappy over the course of my childhood and adolescence. I was afraid of my own shadow and, also for this reason, I never had a friend.

I wasn't doing well in school. Even there, I found discomfort and loneliness.

My teacher Emma was a violent woman, unable to love, I was very afraid of her. I was beaten, kicked and punched by this woman for all five years of elementary school. The physical abuse was so great that I remained immobilized by fear.

TALKING TO ANGELS

I feared the world: my father, my teacher, the classmates who insulted me, the relatives and friends of my family. The world was bad, or the world didn't want me because I didn't deserve to be loved. My only relief valve, my true lifeline, for all his short life, my angel, was my mother. Going home and seeing her smiling at me and my siblings as soon as we entered the door was a wonderful thing for me. Watching her face light up every time her children came home was the most beautiful thing in the world.

My mother was my only lifeline in the ugliness of the world that I lived in from a little boy to adulthood. I can still see her open her arms, crouch down, and welcome us in a big hug. Being bullied and ridiculed by so many was the leitmotiv of my adolescence. For this, I locked myself in solitude: neglected and on the sidelines. I created an impenetrable armor around myself that no one could access except the invisible world to which I opened my heart every night. A fantastic world, a world invisible to others, where I could go whenever I wanted to feel safe and secure. I remember going to bed and seeing angels enter my room. They would take me away to wonderful places. They showed me different countries and many other surreal places. They were preparing me for my life. The angels were my teachers, my invisible brothers and sisters, those who taught me everything in my life. They taught me to be sensitive, inviting me to be kind and caring. They taught me not to get angry, never to shout, not to be upset by the behavior of others and to always forgive people, starting with all those who hurt me. One night, while I was talking to my angels, my father entered my room. I remember he started questioning me.
"Who are you talking to?"
I was petrified. I couldn't answer him. The more he pressed me, the less I replied, and this made him very angry.
He started hitting me hard, until I found the strength to confess: "I talk to angels, Dad."
I guess he was scared or worried, but life became torture. I was visited by psychologists and psychiatrists to see what was wrong with me. I went through all kinds of medical tests. The doctors

found nothing wrong with me, my body or my brain and they told my parents that I had an extraordinary sensitivity.

From that moment, all my extra-sensory experiences stopped abruptly.

I was desperately looking for help but I was alone and too young for an introspective journey. So I searched elsewhere for the protection and satisfaction that no one else was able to give me. Which is how I found my first true, faithful friend. The loyal friend that I could not do without and which allowed me to fill every emptiness and allay all my fears, was food.

Food became an unstoppable and uncontrollable addiction. I would eat, eat and eat some more. I would eat to both punish myself as well as to feel less lonely when it seemed that even my angels had stopped talking to me. After my relationship with the angels had so abruptly ended, I thought only about eating and sleeping, perhaps even dying.

At a later stage, I developed type 2 diabetes. I have since learned that this type of diabetes develops in people who no longer have a zest for life and who do not feel appreciated enough.

It was like that for me.

My father never said 'good' or 'well done' to me. Not even once, not even by mistake. A gesture of approval on his part would have been like touching the sky with a finger, but it never came.

I've waited for this to happen my whole life, and now I know it won't happen.

LONDON CALLING

It took me a long time to forgive him and forgive myself.

Forgiveness is the key to any healing, starting with forgiveness of oneself.

Healing your inner child is an extraordinary experience, an epiphany, a gift from the universe.

When I was aged 17, my parents decided to send me to England for a summer study holiday.

I was fascinated by this country, by its culture and its history. I was fascinated by the language, by Queen Elizabeth and the history of her family. I am still very attracted to English customs and traditions. The respect they have for animals, plants and their gardens. No matter which country, which religion, which culture, which colour, which sexuality, everything is allowed in England and this has always given me a strong feeling of freedom. England has given me back my wings to fly to my faraway nest.

I will always remember the first time I arrived in England: it was like coming home, to a familiar place where I felt I had already been. At that moment I promised myself that I would study English history and literature, since I knew that, one day I would come to live in this country. So I did. And a week after graduating from university, I moved to London.

It was one of the most beautiful and exciting times of my life. London was life, freedom, courage to live and look inside me.

One day I decided to visit Hampton Court Palace, the residence that Cardinal Wolsey had built for his king, Henry VIII. When I got there, I had an unforgettable experience. I knew I had been there before. I don't know when, a previous life? A dream? I didn't know, but I felt I knew that building centimeter by centimeter. I knew I had been there in a previous life, in the time of Henry VIII. Was I the king? A courtier? Was I a servant or a madman? I studied the Tudor period thoroughly and, growing up, I would only buy books on the Tudor era for this inexplicable attraction. Arriving at Hampton Court, the whole image became much clearer. I decided to find a job as a sales clerk in Westminster Abbey, where I sold souvenirs to tourists. Going to this beautiful church every day and being surrounded by so much history gave me a daily dose of inspiration. Life in England marked a new beginning, also for my extrasensory experiences. I felt as if my third eye was finally reopening. My guardian angels, my spiritual guides, directed me towards a new life, a new beginning. Leaving the abbey, I decided to start my translation career. Although I liked very much being able to interact with people from different countries and speak different languages, I soon got tired of it. I was in constant search and my life pushed me towards a dimension in which I finally felt at ease: I decided to buy a house in London. An apartment in Chiswick, West London. It was my small, welcoming and generous sanctuary. That nest that I had been searching for throughout childhood and adolescence was finally mine. It still is. Every time I return from travel, my little flat remains my safe and protected space. In the peace and wonderful energy of my home, everyone can relax and feel welcomed. Safe in my new London home, I still felt incomplete. My conversations with the beyond continued, but I felt the need to know myself better, as well to get to know my invisible interlocutors better. So it was that I started attending the College of Psychic Studies where great mediums and healers taught throughout the year. I attended classes with Arthur Molinary, Robin Wimbow, Gerry March and Ivy Northage. The lessons were on developing mediumship and healing. I nourished my thirst for knowledge through personal and spiritual development.

BOOKSELLER TO REIKI MASTER

I was so interested in these issues that I decided to open an esoteric bookstore in London called The Metaphysical Centre. Through the years of running the bookstore, I met thousands of people, important and ordinary, but above all my interest in Reiki was born. I heard this word everywhere and the more I tried to forget it, the more it entered me. People who came into my shop would say to me, "I come in here, I sit down, just sit around here for a few minutes and relax, you are a natural healer."

I didn't like this word 'healer' at all and I was trying to escape it.

One day, when I was visiting the Body, Mind and Soul fair in London looking for new ideas for the Metaphysical Centre, I met Stefanie. Sitting at her stand with a big smile, as I passed, she asked me: "Why don't you try 10 minutes of Reiki healing with me?" Again that word. Was the universe trying to tell me something? I decided to try it. Stefanie gave me my first treatment. I loved it. In 10 minutes, it had put me into a state of complete relaxation and peace, despite being surrounded by hundreds of people. I immediately enrolled in her first level of Reiki course, which she was holding the following weekend. I felt as if a great portal had opened before me, I had started a new path and it was what my soul was looking for, the source of love that would refresh me. Here it was, the answer to my many questions. Everyone I had met so far had told me I was a great natural healer but that was just a word I didn't like. When Reiki entered my life, all the pieces of the puzzle came together. Reiki saved my life. The Universal Energy that uses me as a channel between Source and the whole world is that tireless energy that heals the evils of the world. The following year, in Sedona in Arizona, in the Rocky Mountains, at William Rand's school, I became a Reiki Master and from there the second part of my life began which was to be of service to others, those most in need of love and attention.

IN SERVICE

As an important part of my service, I began to dedicate my healing work to the terminally ill. It seemed to me that Reiki could be of help to people who were dying and their families. Helping other human beings during the transition to Spirit is an unforgettable experience that I always carry with me.

After the sudden and painful death of my beloved mother, I decided to move to America. Kelly, one of my closest friends, was suffering from cancer and I felt the desire to be close to her and help her in that very difficult moment. Kelly was a bright and effervescent girl from New York. I had met her in Paris while working there as a translator in the early 90s. We spent hours talking and our friendship had grown closer. Like me, Kelly had had a severe and very hard father, especially with words. When our French experience ended, I went back to London and she went back to New York. We continued to talk often on the phone, telling us about our different lives but staying very close, despite not seeing each other for some years. One day Kelly confided to me in tears that she had been diagnosed with ovarian cancer. I didn't think twice; I had to go and stay with her and help her, give her all the support and love she needed at the time. Getting to Colourado and meeting Kelly again brought mixed emotions. On the one hand, the joy of seeing a dear friend; on the other, a stab in the heart when I came face to face again with the girl I'd known from Paris who, back then was full of the desire to live. In the years since then, she had become a thin woman, frail, with long lifeless, gray hair. Thus began my life in Boulder, Colourado, in the Rocky Mountains where Kelly and I took long walks with our dogs. Those chats, immersed in nature, were a dialogue between two souls who had reconnected.

Kelly confided in me about her life growing up that she remembered with feelings of guilt and fear. She told me she'd never felt good enough to have her own family. She told me how scarred she felt inside. Unable to open up to love, she could never find happiness in a relationship. An evil of living, a spiritual evil so intense and indelible that it consumed it deeply, to the point of affecting it in the body.

Kelly left on a snowy January day.

I have not stopped thinking about her sad smile, but I am sure she is doing well in that place where each of us is loved regardless, without judgment.

I learned a lot from that time with Kelly. I understood how much soul wounds can affect our health.

I never thought I could heal her.

I had never healed anyone but myself. You will never hear me say, 'I healed this or that person'. Only God heals so I don't call myself a healer, I am a channeler, if healing is part of the spiritual path of that human being. We are only channels, the rest is energy.

TURNING POINT

In Boulder, I opened my first Reiki clinic, where I worked for three years.

At some point in my journey, I heard the call of home and decided to return to London. From there I went to Naples, India, Pakistan, the Middle East, back to London and then again around the world on my travels. I met hundreds of people on my journey and it is this love that gives meaning and fullness to our existence.

I learn something through every meeting, through every experience, including teaching. And when I teach, I learn to teach myself that that the greatest lesson of life starts from listening to ourselves.

That part of us that we hide and mistreat, we imprison, detest, that asks us to listen and love, like that funny boy from Naples, who detested hunting and spoke with angels.

It all starts from there: being able to forgive and understand deeply first of all ourselves and then others, and to continue to forgive until our hearts are expanded and free.

When I treat someone with Reiki, I am willing to transfer unconditional love. I listen to the other person, trying to understand the soul in front of me and trying to free it.

Here the energy of Reiki manifests itself in those who are willing to welcome it; in those who have opened their hearts to receive this blessing and to start the healing process.

A circular process in which space and time merge, in which I and the OTHER disappear, in which we are US; we are LOVE. We are in that space where we become children again; reborn with

that simple spark that vibrates our soul and connects us to our our guardian angels.
.

CHAPTER TWO

ROOTS OF REIKI

The Reiki we know today was already known in India at the time of Gautama Siddhartha, the man known as the Buddha, who lived between the 6th and 5th centuries BC.

Many of the symbols and processes of Reiki refer to Buddhism, such as the use of the same signs or the laying on of hands, and many of the principles of Buddhist philosophy are covered in Reiki.

In Buddhism, most of the information on healing has been passed down orally. However, if a Master did not consider their students ready, they would not pass on the knowledge, and therefore it's probable that some teachings have been lost. Perhaps this is why there is not a clear explanation of the path of illumination amongst all the material written on Tantric Buddhism (a form of Buddhism that includes spiritual healing of mind, emotions and body).

The traditional story of how Reiki was rediscovered gives the credit to Dr Mikao Usui, (1865-1926) a Japanese scholar who taught in a Christian school of theology.

The story of how Reiki was discovered by Dr Usui was handed down by his pupil Hawayo Takata, but shadows of doubt linger over the veracity of the biographical reconstruction. Studies and research by enthusiasts such as Frank Arjava Petter, a German Reiki therapist who found Usui's tomb in Tokyo, have shown that the Takata narrative does not always hold up against known facts.

This is likely because Takata began to spread Reiki in the aftermath of the Second World War and so she tried to westernize the figure of

Mikao Usui as much as possible, given that the Japanese at that time did not enjoy the esteem of Westerners.

There are two other theories: the first describes Usui as a Japanese Christian monk, director of Doshisha University, a small Catholic university in Kyoto; the other identifies him as a Buddhist monk in Japan.

USUI THE LEGEND

Usui was born on August 15 of the Keio period, which corresponds to 1865. The legendary story goes that, while working as a minister and teacher at a Christian school for boys, one of Usui's students asked him whether he believed in the Bible's stories of Jesus' healing and, if so, when would he teach the boys how to do this type of healing?

It's said that this question lit a fire in Usui's belly and he then dedicated his life to finding out how Jesus and the Buddha were able to heal. Usui have travelled far and wide in search of answers and consulted the original religious texts of Christianity and Buddhism, even learning Sanskrit to do so. Eventually, his search brought him to a Zen Buddhist monastery in Kyoto, Japan. The Abbot of this monastery advised Usui to meditate deeply for his answers.

So Usui undertook a 21-day fasting retreat on nearby Mount Kurama. To keep track of the days, he collected 21 small stones and placed them on the ground within reach of where he sat, with the intention of throwing one away for every day he spent on the mountain.

Nothing happened until the last day of his quest. Early on the morning of the 21st day, Usui saw a ball of light on the horizon coming towards him at great speed.

His first instinct was to run away, but then he decided to surrender to whatever was happening. The ball of light hit him in the centre of the forehead, in his third eye chakra. As soon as he was touched, Usui began to see "millions and millions of rainbow-coloured bubbles". As well, he saw the Reiki symbols, the same sacred symbols that he had studied in the Tibetan scriptures. As he saw these sacred symbols, he received both a deep understanding of each symbol and an attunement, or activation, to their healing energy.

Usui left the sacred mountain with the same knowledge of Buddha and the healer Jesus. He had achieved enlightenment.

Four miracles immediately followed. As Usui rushed back down the mountain in excitement, he injured his foot in his haste. He bent down to hold his toe and the bleeding stopped and the pain went away. As well, he was able to eat normally despite having been fasting for 21 days. He also healed a woman's toothache by placing his hands on the side of her face. Then, on returning to the monastery, he healed his friend the Abbot who was laid up in bed with painful arthritis attacks. Usui realised that he had at last discovered the healing power that he had been so ardently seeking.

The Reiki system we use today evolves from Mikao Usui, which is why it is called the Usui System of Natural Healing, or Usui Shiky Ryoho.

Inspired by his amazing discovery, Usui wanted to use Reiki's healing energy to help others, so he went to the impoverished slums of Kyoto to heal society's most physically unwell people. For several years he lived in the slums and healed the town's beggars, urging them to leave begging and begin a new life. He encouraged them to improve their lives and get out of the poverty in which they found themselves.

Over time, though, Usui was disappointed and dismayed to see the people he had healed returning back to the slums. They claimed that life in the 'outside' world was much more difficult, eventually preferring to stay in the slums to beg, even though they were no longer ill or deformed.

This discouraged Usui greatly and, disconsolate, he returned to his monastery.

His experience in the Kyoto slums made Usui realise that it was not possible to heal the body if you did not also heal the heart and spirit. Usui ceased his work in the slums and instead started travelling throughout Japan, going from village to village to offer teaching and healing.

In every village, he would stand on a street corner with a small lit torch. To anyone who stopped to ask him was he was doing, he would reply that he was looking for those people who wanted to better themselves and who wanted healing.

In this way, he spent many years teaching and healing around Japan, although he made it clear that it was not he who was doing the healing; that it was God's energy passing through him.

As well as offering healing, he concentrated on teaching others how to heal so that people could be empowered in their own lives. Usui is said to have initiated 16 Masters in Reiki, one of whom was Dr Chujiro Hayashi (1879-1940). Hayashi took over the work of spreading his teachings after Usui's death in 1926.

USUI THE MAN

Beyond the legendary stories, the true story of Usui is that he was born on 15 August 1865 in the village of Yago, in the Yamagata district, in the prefecture of Gifu.

According to the memorial on his gravestone, it is known that he was a learned scholar and that he traveled extensively throughout Japan and visited China and the western world.

After his spiritual enlightenment and his initiation into Reiki on Mount Kurama, Usui started doing Reiki on himself and his relatives. He had married a woman called Sadako of the Suzuki family. In the years between 1908 and 1910, the couple had a son named Fuji and a daughter named Toshiko, .

He then opened a clinic in Harajuku, in Ojama, Tokyo, in April of the eleventh year of the Taisho period (1922).

In 1923, there was a terrible and devastating earthquake in Tokyo. In the aftermath, Usui went through the streets of the city to bring comfort and Reiki to the desperate.

In February 1925, he built a new clinic in Nakano near Tokyo, and over time he became famous throughout Japan. Many people travelled to his clinic for healing.

He traveled a lot and it was during one of these trips, to Fukuyama in March 1926, that Usui died of a stroke. He was aged 60 in Western terms and 62 in old Japan style, which counts you as age one at birth and then you turn another year older at the start of the new year.

Usui was neither a Christian monk, nor a Buddhist monk, but he was a cultured and curious man, and a practicing Buddhist from the Pure Land Buddhist school.

According to his memorial headstone, Usui was mild, gentle and humble by nature although physically he was big and strong. He had many talents and a deep knowledge of history, biographies, medicine, theological books like Buddhism Kyoten and different scriptures, psychology, jinsen no jitsu, ju jitsu, incantations, the science of divination, physiognomy and the I Ching. His peers and students thought that Usui's training in these different disciplines gave him the foundations for being able to perceive Reiki.

CHAPTER THREE

THE MASTERS LINEAGE

CHUJIRO HAYASHI

Dr Chujiro Hayashi was a retired Imperial Navy officer. On meeting Usui, Hayashi was immediately struck by his sincerity and began traveling with his Master, assisting him in his lectures.

In 1925, Hayashi also became a Reiki therapist. In 1926, Usui named Hayashi as his successor. He had initiated a total of 16 masters, although official sources only recognise Hayashi.

Hayashi opened the Shina Nomaci clinic in Tokyo and instructed a group of his collaborators to work in groups, offering healing to patients, or going to the homes of those who could not move. He developed the use of specific positions and the system of three teaching levels, each with its own initiation processes. He also introduced the accepting of cash payments for Reiki treatments.

HAWAYO TAKATA

In 1935, a Hawaiian woman named Hawayo Takata (1900-1980) arrived at Hayashi's clinic to receive healing for a serious tumour, having refused to undergo surgery. Takata was cured in just four months. As a result, she was so impressed by Reiki that she wanted to learn it immediately. Initially, Hayashi refused to give her lessons because she was a foreign woman (he wanted to keep Reiki only in Japan), but at her imploring, he eventually changed his mind and Takata received her First Level of Reiki in 1936.

She worked in Hayashi's clinic for a year and then received the second level. In 1937, Takata returned home to Hawaii where she opened her own clinic. In 1938, Chujiro Hayashi went to Hawaii to promote Reiki and, while there, he taught Takata the teachings of the Third Level of Discipline and suggested to her that payment should be made for healing sessions.

By now, the war was near and Hayashi was afraid that he would be called back to fight, kill and make war against other human beings, which was absolutely contrary to his spiritual growth. Hayashi was also afraid that the teachings of Reiki would be lost with the coming war, so he transferred his world leadership to Takata and also decided to end his life. Not wanting to be forced to kill others, Hayashi is said to have stopped his heart with psychic methods.

THE 22 MASTERS

Reiki continued through Takata and it was she who popularized Reiki in the west. During the last 10 years of her life, Takata trained 22 Reiki masters before she died in 1980.

In 1983, a group of Reiki masters founded the Reiki Alliance and appointed Phyllis Lei Furumoto, Takata's granddaughter, as Grand Master and Lineage Bearer. In 1988, Phyllis authorized other Reiki masters, with at least three years of experience, to initiate new masters. Since Takata's death, there have been many changes in the teachings of Reiki. Among these changes have been the development of new techniques, including those by Phyllis Lei Furumoto.

Although I respect various Reiki associations around the world, I consider myself an independent Reiki Therapist.

Here are the 22 Masters initiated by Hawayo Takata:

1 George Araki
2 Dorothy Baba
3 Ursula Baylow

4 Rick Bockner
5 Barbara Brown
6 Fran Brown
7 Patricia Ewing
8 Phyllis Furumoto
9 Beth Gray
10 John Gray
11 Iris Ishikuro
12 Harry Kuboi
13 Ethel Lombardi
14 Barbara McCullough
15 Mary McFadyen
16 Paul Mitchell
17 Bethel Phaigh
18 Barbara Ray
19 Virginia Samdhal
20 Shimobu Saito
21 Seiji Takimori
22 Wanja Twan

All the Reiki Masters in the western world today can trace their lineage back to one of these 22 people initiated by Takata. However, Usui's Reiki also continues in Japan.

CHAPTER FOUR

Usui's Legacy

The issue of Usui's and Takata's legacy has been highly controversial and hotly debated by the Masters who survived the latter's death.
Carell Ann Farmer, who was the fourth teacher initiated by Phyllis Furumoto, was present both at the meeting of the first Masters in 1982 and at the meeting to form the Reiki Alliance in 1983. She wrote the following letter on 31 December 1997 and has given permission for anyone to make copies of this letter to share with others.

Dear Reiki Masters,
I am writing this letter to share my truth in response to the present events that surround the practice of Reiki, in particular, the design of Office of the Grand Master, the concept of a sole and rightful heir, lineage bearer, trademarking and licensing.

I write to provide a more complete picture of the growth of the Usui System of Reiki. I write because I have the courage and understanding now to do so. I write to encourage other people to speak their truth. I write so that I can honour the life force as it lives within me.
I was trained by Phyllis Furumoto in January, 1981 in the first two levels of Reiki. During my 1st level seminar, I received three gifts: the knowing that I was a teacher of this natural healing art (it was known then as Reiki - A Japanese Natural Healing Art), the knowing that it was an individual path and that my inner wisdom would always guide

me, the knowing that when I touched healing happened. The actualization of this wisdom has strengthened over the ensuing years with the challenges presented to me.

I was initiated as a Reiki Master on April 1, 1982. I was the fourth Reiki Master that Phyllis initiated. I paid Phyllis $10,000. Phyllis asked me to make two commitments: to honour Reiki as an oral tradition and for it to be my sole source of income. I committed. I also committed to bringing forth the master in me. I have upheld my commitment to the oral tradition. At the time of making that commitment I did not really understand what it meant to commit to an oral tradition. I was a single parent with two children and no other source of income. It was a huge leap of faith to trust that the universe would totally provide all that I needed to raise and provide for my family. My work as a teacher of natural healing and my life have been supported by this practice. I have been invited to travel extensively to give seminars and treatments. It has been a profound experience of support and love. It has taught me the essence of Reiki. I have upheld the commitment to it being my sole source of income. On April 1, 1996, I took my healing work into the corporate world, where I have gained experience and strength in standing strong in the face of politics and the bottom line of making a profit. I live the practice quietly and continue to deepen my understanding of what it is to follow my inner wisdom and to dedicate my life to mastery.

Some of the memories that I want to share are parts of conversations that Phyllis had with me during my seminars in the first two levels of Reiki, my subsequent training as a Reiki Master and my friendship with her that extended over several years. I have held these conversations in confidence based on my personal ethics. The interactive relationship with Phyllis no longer exists and that is of my choosing. I have felt for many years that I cannot align with the control and power which she exerts in her role. Phyllis and I were strong catalysts for each other. We each have our own destiny to fulfill. As in all relationships, we have the right to agree and disagree. I want to state clearly that I have no interest in making Phyllis appear 'wrong' for her choices. I wish only to speak from my heart and some of what I have to say is in disagreement with her choices. It was a difficult path for me because she was my teacher and friend. I was taught that one of the Reiki precepts was to honour one's teacher.

I met Phyllis shortly after her grandmother, Hawayo Takata died. Over a period of several years (1981 - 1984) we were in close association. Phyllis confided in me. She talked to me in great detail of her confusion over her grandmother's death, her grandmother's lack of clarifying Phyllis's future role, her lack of direction in her own life and her fear of the opportunity that was before her to step forward into the position that her grandmother had filled.

I remember the day that she arrived at my house and pronounced that she had made a decision. Her decision was clear. She said, "I will go for the money." She had decided to pursue her grandmother's work - teaching classes, initiating Masters - for the income potential. She initiated four Masters between February 1981 and April 1982. She began to plan the first gathering of Reiki Masters in Hawaii (April 1982) and the memorial service for her grandmother. In many ways, she was already acting as though she was walking in her grandmother's shoes.

Her statement of "I will go for the money" impacted me deeply. It felt wrong to me given my own experience of Reiki. Even though I was a neophyte, I had felt the depth inherent in Reiki. I had felt the spiritual impact.

Her decision was a materialistic decision. In my experience, there was no spiritual awareness associated with it and I felt the paradox of that. My confusion regarding 'honouring my teacher' deepened.

I sat in the circle at the first gathering of Reiki Masters in Hawaii in 1982. I had been an initiated Master for 10 days. I listened to the stories of how Takata had taught each master differently. We drew the symbols together. It was quite shocking to the group to find out that they were different, similar in some respects and different in others. What did this mean? Discussion around this led to an agreement that we would all use the same symbols. I no longer remember exactly how we determined the correct symbols. It marked the beginning of attempted standardization. Takata's unique method of teaching was a source of great upset. We did not understand the uniqueness and came to it with our Western notion of uniformity and standardization. It was not apparent from the discussion that anyone in the group understood the real relationship of the symbols as a catalyst for inner awakening and connection to the Energy. If this had been understood at the time, we would not have engaged in the process of needing to have everyone's symbols be exactly the same. Is this understood now? Do we understand that Takata's way of teaching allowed each master freedom to discover their own uniqueness? Do we understand that each Master is unique?

I also heard the confusion. No successor had been named. Barbara Weber was representing herself as the next leader. This was a source of concern because she had taken actions and was making claims about some agreements with Takata. Also, she had been invited to participate in the gathering and had declined. Phyllis was questioned about what Takata had said to her before she died. Phyllis said that her grandmother had hoped that she would follow in her footsteps, but that she had not said anything definitive about it. Phyllis was questioned about any additional knowledge or symbols that Takata had given her. She did not have any. But she was the only person that had started to initiate masters in the group. She was in many ways leading the gathering. She said that she was open to being chosen as the person who would follow in Takata's footsteps and eventually that is what appeared to happen. It seemed that nobody wanted the responsibility of the role except Phyllis and nobody really understood what was to happen. I think that we did not have a glimmer of understanding of how Reiki could have moved forward without a 'leader'.

At that gathering, I received another profound gift. I had a powerful experience regarding the concept of grand master. I knew from deep within my being that I had the potential of being a grand master. I had just been initiated as a Master. I was the 'baby' in the group. The possibility of envisioning myself embodying the concept of grand master or the notion of speaking that I had that profound inner knowing was ludicrous and terrifying. I chose not to speak of it.

I wish that I had had the courage and trust of my heart to speak. It could have made a great difference to the future of Reiki. It is clear to me that if I had spoken, it would have initiated a discussion about the concept of "grand master." The future of the Usui System of Reiki may have looked very different. Consider for a moment a discussion about the concept of "grand master" amongst those Reiki masters. "Grand master", not as a title or a position, but as a possibility that each and every one of us can aspire to. I believe that at some level everyone at that gathering had this energy experience of the potential of grand mastery. I know that as one of the participants, I felt that energy through my body and I felt the full force and potential of that awareness. I know that we all have the opportunity to direct our lives to grand mastery. We could be living in the question "What is grand mastery"? A powerful spiritual focus that is our birth right. To live in this question is quite different from acting as if we are "grand masters". If there is a designation or honouring with a title, I believe that it must be earned from living an exemplary life.

It seems to me that everyone has forgotten the naivete of the participants at the meeting. It was the first time that a group of Reiki

Masters had sat together in America. We were all essentially 'babies' in our practice of Reiki. We were dealing with issues that required wisdom and maturity in the practice of Reiki. I don't feel that we even began to understand that at the time. The lack of understanding of succession, the confusion over Takata's method of teaching, the variations in the symbols, the threat that Barbara Weber would fill the gap provided by Takata's death were expressed fears within the group. Nobody there knew the decision that Phyllis had made "to go for the money," except me and I did not share that information. None of the people present took the fact that Takata had not designated a successor to mean that there was not to be a successor. It is possible that this is the truth.

A further development happened at the next gathering of Reiki Masters, which was held at Barbara Brown's home in British Columbia in 1983. The Reiki Alliance was formed. I can no longer recall exact details. I remember that Phyllis was acting as the leader and most persons there moved with the energy of the situation. I remember spending days working on the purpose statement of the Reiki Alliance. It was the beginning of the further westernization of Reiki. As people born and raised in the West, we have a certain set of values and definitions. When these definitions and values are applied to a set of values and definitions from another culture, they change the original meaning. In the case of Reiki, I think that we have deviated greatly from the original teaching and intent. It requires intensive study and contemplation to understand a different culture. The only way we had of understanding was through our Western mind set. This Western way of thinking coupled with Phyllis's own motivation led to her being known as Grand Master and later, her proclamation of being a lineage bearer and now, that she is the sole and rightful heir of the Usui System of Reiki. I do not think that what transpired was in the energy of the system itself, rather an outcome of the Western way and Phyllis's ambition.

At the next gathering of the Reiki Alliance, one of the Masters asked Phyllis to talk about what happened when Takata died and the process of how she came to claim to be a successor. She began to tell a story that was a fabrication. I called for truth. Phyllis retracted her statements, but the question remained unanswered. After that gathering, I left the Reiki Alliance. I felt that Phyllis had created a fabrication around the Usui System of Reiki that was a protection for her own purposes. I began to walk my own path with Reiki. I began the process of following my inner wisdom.

For the past seventeen years, I have been deepening my understanding and integrating those first three gifts from my first level seminar and the fourth gift from my sitting in the circle in Hawaii in 1982. Those spiritual experiences have been my guides in this journey. It is a blessing in my life that they have led to greater and greater simplicity and love.

I do not align with the complex notions that are currently expressed by Phyllis about this practice. I do not align with any of the notions of a role of grandmaster, office of grandmaster, lineage bearer, sole and rightful heir of the Usui System of Reiki or licensing fees for Masters because they do not come from the system itself. What is all this for? Who benefits from all this 'stuff?' It looks to me like Phyllis does. The notions of form, discipline and practice are inherent in the way that this healing art is presented by the Reiki Master. At least at one time this was true. In the oral tradition, the emphasis was on self-discovery and embodied in the concept 'allow the Energy to lead you'. There is no need to have lengthy treatises about it. Trust the Reiki Master to live it and model it. It is simple. It exists.

We are all lineage bearers, rightful heirs and potentially grandmasters. It is not the exclusive right of one person.

We have a great opportunity to free ourselves from confusion and return to the true simplicity of this gentle practice. I believe that we have the maturity and understanding at this time to speak, to be heard and bring forth the dignity and integrity of this teaching. We are all responsible for what has happened and we are all responsible for the future.

To be a Reiki Master is to hold a sacred trust. This purity of heart is the essence of what we have to share. I pray that together we can bring that purity forth to clarify the past, live what we teach and teach what we live.

I send you this letter with love and blessings,
Carell Ann Farmer

CHAPTER FIVE

FIVE PRINCIPLES OF REIKI

Several years after founding Reiki, Usui was inspired during a meditation one day to add the Five Principles of Reiki (Gokai) into the training and philosophy of the discipline.

The five Reiki principles derive in part from the Five Principles of Emperor Meiji, whom Usui admired. The Reiki principles were developed to achieve spiritual balance. Their purpose is to help people realise that spiritual healing is made possible by consciously deciding to improve oneself, which is a necessary part of the Reiki healing experience.

In order for Reiki to have long-lasting results, clients must accept responsibility for their own wellness and actively take part in their own healing process.

Therefore, Usui's Reiki method is more than just the use of Reiki energy because it must include an active commitment to improve oneself.

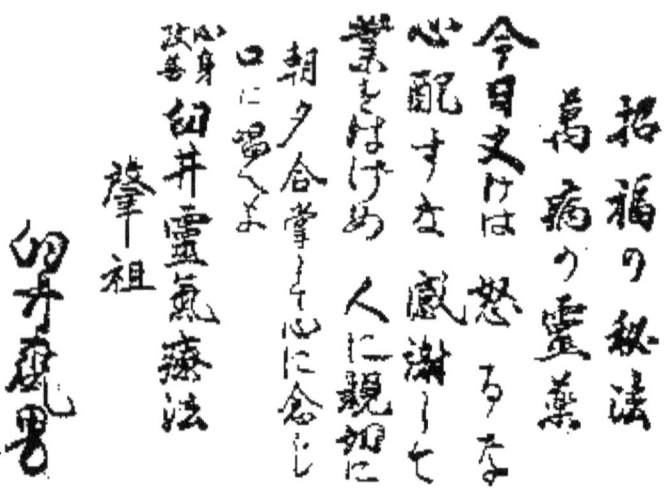

The secret art of inviting happiness
The miraculous medicine of all diseases
Just for today, do not anger
Do not worry and be filled with gratitude
Do your work honestly. Be kind to people.
Every morning and evening, join your hands in prayer.
Pray these words to your heart
and chant these words with your mouth
Usui Reiki Treatment for the improvement of body and mind
The founder, Mikao Usui

USUI'S FIVE PRINCIPLES

Mikao Usui himself wrote that the five principles (*Gokai*) were: *'The secret art of inviting blessings, the spiritual medicine of all diseases.'*

Shoufuku no hihoo - The secret method of inviting blessings.
Manbyo no Reiyaku - The wonderful medicine for all diseases.
Kyo dake wa - Just for today.

The five principles are:

1 - Okoruna - Don't be angry.
2 - Shimpai suna - Don't worry.
3 - Kansha shite - Be thankful.
4 - Goo hage me - Work diligently (on yourself).
5 - Hito ni shinsetsu ni - Be kind to others.

"Asa yuu Gassho shite, kokoro ni nenji, kuchi ni tonaeyo. Shin shin kaizen." Usui Reiki Ryoho Chosso Usui Mikao

"Every morning and evening, sitting in the Gassho position (with hands joined in prayer), pray these words to your heart and chant these words with your mouth. For the evolution of body and soul." Usui Reiki Ryoho. The founder Mikao Usui

Just for today do not get angry.
Just for today do not worry.
Just for today work diligently and honestly.
Just for today honour your Masters, parents and the elderly.
Just for today be thankful for all living things.

All principles start with 'Just for today', which highlights one of the foundations of Reiki: living fully in the present.

It is the *'hic et nunc'* (here and now) that pervaded Western and Eastern philosophy. In other words, to look for a way of living our day-to-day life that enables us to fully experience life without meaningless nostalgia and without delaying our choices and decisions.

Living 'just for today' means not succumbing to the fear and anxiety that makes modern people lead busy, stressful lives, without being able to stop and take in the beauty of the world, nor listen to the breathing of the Earth.

Living 'just for today' means not mulling over past hurts, anger and worries that give rise to hate and acrimony, which then settle in the soul and bring about negative feelings.

Living 'just for today' means respecting universal laws and people, and being grateful for all the experiences and the people we've encountered on our journey.

1. 'Just for today, I do not get angry'

Anger is one of the most devious emotions the human soul can experience, because it is not always easy to identify. Often, it hides behind other emotions, such as fear or vengefulness or is turned inwards and becomes apathy or depression.

Therefore, it is important to recognise anger and face it for what it is. Feelings of anger should not be repressed as this can lead to physical illness as well as mental disorder. It's important to recognise the mechanisms that lead to anger and also face life understanding and being compassionate towards oneself first of all.

2. 'Just for today, I do not worry'

Worries sweep across our soul virtually every single minute of our existence, because we cannot give our life a sense of direction, we

cannot firmly hold the helm. We are lacking in self-confidence and we are unsure of our destiny so we let fear wear us out.
Surrendering to a higher power and releasing the need to try and control everything is how this principle should be followed.

3. 'Just for today, I work diligently'

This principle is based on the honesty and diligence that guides us in the way we do our work but also in our everyday actions. Honesty means looking at other people and our reflection in the mirror with profound dignity and respect.

4. 'Just for today, I honour my Masters, my parents, my ancestors, my elders.'

Respect for our elders and for one's parents is one of the foundations of the natural laws of every culture.
Respect for those who gave us life but also for our ancestors; those who came before us and devoted themselves and their work to the community. We should honour all those who showed us the way because teaching life is a difficult and complex task.

5. 'Just for today, I am grateful for every living thing.'

Being grateful for the immensity of the universe, and for the great gift of belonging to a group of beings that are part of the circle of existence, is the foundation of the last principle.
Reiki is founded on gratitude, When we practice Reiki, we also move closer to our body and to the things that populate our day-to-day life with respect and gratitude.
All beings come into this world and live in an original and unique way, thanks to our different characters, attitudes and abilities. Each of us

experiences situations, traumas and joy differently from others. Throughout our lives, we make choices and we experience difficult or exciting times.

We cannot know what lies ahead of us and we cannot change the past but we can live in the 'here and now' and use this awareness to walk our path and start our journey of light.

Thanks to Reiki, we can bring light to our life and as well embark on a journey of consciousness and healing in order to brighten other people's lives.

Reiki is always based exclusively on love and on being of service to others. It can be used to heal the body, the mind and the soul, but – most importantly - to improve life.

The Reiki therapist will always draw on the five principles of Reiki every time universal energy is channelled.

CHAPTER SIX

REIKI AS SPIRITUAL ENERGY

Evolution of the word Reiki in Japanese

Old (Pre-1940s) Kanji   Modern Kanji   Modern Katakana

This is the ideogram (kanji) of Rei and Ki, traced with the Kaisho calligraphy that dates back to the sixth dynasty. The two characters that make up the ideogram describe the one. Usually translated as 'Universal Life-force Energy', the word is divided into two parts:

Rei - spiritual energy; intelligence of the universe
Ki – life-force energy that flows through every living thing

The two are inseparable powers that work in unison. They mark heaven and earth, the soul and the body.

Reiki energy is therefore composed of an otherworldly aspect that's linked to the universe, as well as a vital human and bodily element.

In the written character, we find the continuous reference to the Body-Soul-Heart triad. Spirit and matter united by energy that finally heals the dichotomy between body and soul, between mind and heart.

Reiki has a vertical dimension that is marked when the practitioner channels energy and brings it from the universe to the individual, but also a horizontal dimension in the sharing of energy from individual to individual, and between individuals and the world.

The vertical dimension is fully satisfied by the action of the practitioner who, with their therapeutic touch, allows the energy to pass through the recipient's body via their hands, which channel pure and purifying energy from a higher force that here I am calling the universe.

The Reiki energy that the Master channels is a powerful and intelligent purifying energy. This energy works to sweep out all the 'junk' energy that has somehow accumulated in the recipient's body, but which is no longer needed or helpful. This intelligent energy knows where to go and what to do.

The horizontal dimension is given by the human touch, which transmits warmth and feelings of tenderness and love. Healing through Reiki causes us to return to a state of alignment with our super-consciousness; our true being. The Reiki therapist, therefore, receives the energy and channels it through their own hands into the recipient's body.

A sense of total well-being is normally perceived when working on the different energy centres of the body. Indeed, Reiki acts on both the mental and physical bodies.

Reiki is one of the most beautiful gifts that one can receive and share with others. Reiki is universal love, compassion, harmony and balance, and this leads us to perceive a sense of integrity in a path of joy and happiness.

The person who gives Reiki, experiences an expansion of their Ki, their life force, and will often feel energised by this experience. So much so that they can perform Reiki treatments on different clients, one after the other.

The energies of the Reiki practitioner are never depleted because Reiki energy is a channeled energy and does not come from the therapist themself - it comes through them. At the same time, the practitioner does not absorb any negative energy from the person being treated. In fact, this negative energy is eliminated through the extremities of the receiver. It is swept out through the soles of their feet as well as out through their hands and fingers.

After being initiated, each Reiki practitioner will be in contact with universal energy for the rest of their life.

As we said, negative thoughts and feelings of resentment are among the main reasons that the flow of Ki energy in our bodies becomes restricted. This is supported by the fact that the mind is responsible for most diseases in the modern world.

Reiki, as a holistic biotechnology, works directly on the subconscious mind, which is where we hold these limiting or negative thoughts, beliefs and feelings. This energy breaks this chain, or vicious circle, and sends the junk energies out of our body.

With these 'blocks' removed, the Ki energy will therefore be free to flow, thus rebalancing physiological functions and restoring optimal psychophysical health conditions.

To describe this using a metaphor, we can say that what happens for those who receive a Reiki treatment is akin to thinking of a dark house in which all the lights magically turn on.

The switches, which are connected to the lightbulbs and lamps, represent the chakras. The chakras connect the physical body to the super-consciousness. These lights require repairs and must be tested to ensure that there are no blockages to the flow of electricity, also known as energy.

Therefore, the chakras in our body need to be rebalanced in order to let the vital energy flow properly. Once the switches - chakras - are cleared of obstructions and faulty connections are repaired, then the electricity itself - Reiki Energy - is able to flow freely to ensure that your home - body - can turn back on and that light can reach every room.

The body is the *trait d'union,* or link, between Rei and Ki: if Rei is spirituality and Ki physicality, energy must flow from one to the other and the channel through which it flows is, in fact, the body.

The body is attached to the ground but is reaching towards Heaven and is in a circuit of energy that goes from Earth to Heaven, through the forces of liberation and from Heaven to Earth, thanks to the forces of manifestation.

If there are no energy blocks to jam this current, it is a continuous and harmonious flow.

An emotional block causes trouble because it slows down this continuous flow of energy and upsets the system of spiritual communication that a person has with themselves as well as with the universe.

If the emotional blocks are not resolved, they clog the circuit and create an imbalance that passes from Rei to Ki. This creates malaise; an emotional discomfort that, if left unresolved, becomes a physical issue.

A Reiki treatment rebalances the flow of energy and dissolves the blocks. Information about the body's discomfort is passed to the mind, which recognizes and can thus process the reasons for the imbalance.

So, since receiving Reiki treatments is so important and beneficial, as a trainer and practitioner, my hope is that a pact will be created between students, who, in addition to giving Reiki, can exchange treatments with each other.

If you create a partnership with others in your group, you have the opportunity to achieve important results in your own spiritual healing. As well as the gift of friendship with those who are walking this same path.

CHAPTER SEVEN

How Reiki Works

Since Reiki is guided by an intelligent force, both the mind and experience of the therapist do not contaminate the universal energy.
The therapist or practitioner is a channel of universal energy and in the moment, this therapist makes room in their body to allow the divine energies to enter within.
During treatment, the therapist receives an expansion of Ki, which leads them to feel energised and able to perform even more treatments one after the other.
The therapist's energies will never run out because they come from the infinite supply of universal force.
The Reiki therapist does not absorb any energy from the client. In fact, the client's old energy is expelled through their extremities (fingers and toes).
This is the essential difference between Reiki and Pranotherapy. Basically, Pranotherapy draws on the energy inherent in the human body, while Reiki utilises universal energy.
The main cause of restriction in the flow of Ki energy through the body is thoughts and feelings of resentment. The mind is responsible for most diseases in the modern world.
Reiki works directly on the subconscious that contains these thoughts and feelings and breaks this vicious circle by sending negative thoughts away forever.

After this phase of 'elimination', the Ki is free to flow in the body, balancing the functions of the physical body and restoring optimal health conditions.

If you think of a house full of lights, the initiation, or attunement, process is nothing more than the action of turning on the house lights. The switches that are connected to the lights represent the chakras.

The chakras connect the physical body to super consciousness. These lights require repairs and must be tested to ensure there are no blockages to the flow of energy.

Likewise the chakras in our body need to be balanced by the Ki to flow properly. Once the switches (chakras) are cleared of obstructions, the electricity itself (Universal Energy) will flow freely and cause your home (body) to light up again.

After being initiated, each individual will be in contact with the Universal Energy for the rest of their life.

Every sentient being that comes into this world lives a unique existence thanks to our different characteristics, attitudes and abilities.

Each of us faces our own situations, traumas and joys differently from others. In life we make choices and we come across difficult or stimulating moments.

We cannot know what awaits us and we cannot change the past, but we can live in the here and now and from this awareness, we can face the path of life and start on a path of Light.

Thanks to Reiki you can cast light on your life and embark on a path of awareness and healing that can also improve the lives of others.

Reiki is always and is only based on Love. It is about giving oneself to others and can be used to treat the body, mind and soul, but above all to improve life.

When you give a treatment to yourself or to any other living creature, you open yourself up to the Energy and its subtle vibration will flood your life. When this happens, you will find solutions or paths ahead that remained hidden before.

CHAPTER EIGHT

HOLOGRAPHIC UNIVERSE

The Universe is a hologram of energy fields.
Groundbreaking physicist David Bohm called it a "holographic universe" that we cannot fully know. Our own brain works like a hologram.
We create holograms with our thoughts that can influence the world around us.
When we project our thoughts onto another person, that person is influenced and affected by the energy that our thoughts bring. If these thoughts are cruel or unfair, then those people will become that image we projected onto them.
Here are two statements that allow you to correct these forms of negative energies:

"With this, I now end, remove and delete all the images projected onto me by every person, and by myself, in every time, place and dimension.

"With this, I now finish, remove and delete all the images that I projected onto other people, and onto myself, in every time, place and dimension."

The energy, which gives us life and flows through us thanks to the chakras and the meridians (nadis), lives in our aura and is sensitive to thoughts and feelings. Therefore, if we experience, consciously or unconsciously, negative thoughts or feelings about ourselves, we project them into our aura and clog our own chakras.

Thanks to Reiki, the vibratory level of the energy field in and around the physical body can be raised to clear and restore the free flow of energy.

Negative thought-forms influence our life and represent the lowest level of energy vibrations. The human body mediates what is expressed through the subconscious and transforms the creations of the mind into material forms.

This is why it is necessary to structure our thought-forms in a constructive way, and in harmony with the divine plan, in order to elevate ourselves.

There are also additional levels of the human body that we are less aware of and that vibrate at a higher frequency than the physical body. These levels represent the emotional, mental and spiritual bodies.

1. The physical body is characterized by exercise, awareness of the parts of the body and its functions, touch, importance of nature, elements of earth and water.
2. The emotional body is characterized by fears, doubts, self-expression, openness to joy and happiness.
3. The mental body is characterized by the use of the mind to achieve one's goals, calm thoughts and inner serenity.
4. The spiritual body is characterized by focus on an evolution and on a spiritual path; the path of the soul.

The different levels of Reiki aim to harmonise the various parts of which the human being is composed. The first level harmonises the physical and the emotional bodies; the second level harmonises the emotional body with the mental body, and the third level combines the mental body with the spiritual body.

The first level – called *Shoden*, which means 'first teaching' - guides you to get in touch with your inner self and provides a course in which the principles, history, positions and self-treatment are illustrated.

The second level is called *Okuden*, which means 'deep knowledge'. This level brings you into deep contact with your soul and during this course you learn three Reiki Symbols and how to do distance treatments.

The third level is called *Shinpiden*, which means 'the inner temple'. This level joins the first two floors and introduces the Symbol of the Master. That's why Level Three involves several years of training. During this time, the Reiki Master teaches the student how to make energy flow through their body and how to get in touch with the Universal Laws.

Usui himself said that Reiki was a spiritual secret; a spiritual healing, but also a physical discipline, because energy needs the body through which to flow.

CHAPTER NINE

REIKI IS SERVICE

I decided to provide some testimonials from my students in order to offer a different, albeit subjective perspective of how I experience Reiki first-hand and how I try to pass it on to those with whom I come into contact during my courses. It is certainly a less orthodox way of talking about Reiki, but evidently no less important, given that those who work with Reiki want to target their hearts. Moreover, during my courses, after the time dedicated to theory and practice, a fundamental part is the space dedicated to sharing one's feelings and experiences. It is during these moments that the purest and most true emotions come out, which is a profoundly healing experience.

As has been happening for some time in America, England and Holland, successful initiatives have been undertaken in Italy in hospitals and private clinics. These initiatives are aimed at offering Reiki to support conventional medicine. Personally, my life is dedicated to Reiki and to spreading this simple Japanese method of relaxation and healing in order to help those people who feel they want to improve their lives and dedicate time to their spiritual growth.

Unfortunately, especially in my home country of Italy, this can sometimes translate into a real battle against a misunderstanding, even distrust, of Reiki.

Reiki is not a religion and those who practice it do not belong to a sect. Reiki is nothing but love. True love. Love of the soul, which makes you feel good and makes everyone love. This is why you don't need special skills to be a Reiki practitioner. Everyone can become one. Reiki practitioners are only pure channels, or conduits, of energy. A Reiki practitioner can do many treatments a day, since every time they channel energy for a person, they are themselves purified by the Universal Energy.

The person who performs a Reiki treatment experiences an increase in Ki (Universal Energy); feels energised and can perform several treatments in succession. This experience is unique and varies from treatment to treatment. Many people describe it as very relaxing and soothing. Certainly, the goal of treatment is the mental and physical well-being of the recipient. It helps increase the immunodeficiency system, can eliminate physical pain and minor ailments. Reiki also helps in healing insomnia problems, lack of confidence and helps free people from stress and anxiety.

There are no particular rules for the profession of Reiki practitioner, except for certain ethical and conscientious parameters.

I teach each of the first and second Reiki levels over a weekend, usually in 16-hour masterclasses. The third level of Reiki, which leads to becoming a Reiki Master Teacher, is a longer and more rigorous path.

It is a spiritual path that lasts three years and allows the student to learn, not only Reiki techniques and procedures, but also those of other spiritual disciplines.

It is significant and interesting how one of my students describes her encounter with Reiki:

"Reiki has made my life better and it is with infinite love and gratitude that today I thank all the circumstances of my life, even the most painful ones, that enabled us to get this far and to be able to share my journey with as many wonderful people, who are my soul mates on this extraordinary journey."

The Reiki Master's role is to communicate to others a message of love, energy and beauty of the Universe. In other words, to pass on the same message that they once received. The Master is tasked with revealing to each of their students, the method that will enable them to channel the energy, first for healing themself and then for the healing of others. In doing so, it gives everyone the ability to look within themselves and open the doors of their being so that the subtle and higher energies can flow.

In this way, the Reiki Master has a maieutic[1] function, because thanks to the initiations and the teachings of the three levels, the student is brought to a deeper awareness of themselves and their role in the world.

Here is another testimony from one of my students that opens the heart:

"Each of us is traveling on a pilgrimage in this life that starts from the majestic fragility of being a child.

"We carry that child throughout our existence: it is within us and is weak because it is small, but also powerful because it is close to the whisper of the Universe and capable of achieving great things.

"It is that child who must be reached and who will give us the strength to channel the energy of Reiki.

Our inner child is hidden under fears and emotions, which are the burden that weighs us down and that often makes us sick. Reaching out

---

[1] Maieutic means 'mid-wifery' in the sense of assisting the birth of new ideas. The Maieutic Method offered by ancient Greek philosophers Socrates and Plato is a technique for positively eliciting knowledge in the mind of a person through questioning and discussion.

to the inner child is often the means to relieve yourself of the weight of everyday life.
The journey can be tiring and often it can happen that you stumble or even want to go back. The Master's task, therefore, is to support and encourage the students through this process as necessary.
The prevailing culture of our society, dedicated to production and hyperactivity, often takes us away from spiritual research, which takes time and calm. And this, at times, takes us away from the path that Reiki has laid down before us.I'"

Reiki, as we have already said, is to give love to ourselves first and then to others. However, especially when we give it to ourselves, it is important to establish close contact with our body and organs. That's why during self-treatment, I always recommend to my students that they speak with their organs, such as the lungs, liver or pancreas; to ask questions and let the answers flow in response, welcoming them with an open heart.

It is no coincidence that all treatments begin by focusing attention on the heart chakra. We start by placing our hands on the heart area, first the right hand and then the left, to consciously welcome Universal Energy (Rei-Ki) within us.

It's like pressing a button so we can listen to the flow of energy from the source of life within us. Gradually, with slow and soft steps, placing one hand at a time, we put our hands on our face letting ourselves be accompanied by a sweet, mellow music.

We place our hands on the face, giving all the energy of the universe to our cheeks and therefore to our mouth, jaws and teeth, which help us to grind the food we eat every day. Let's energise this part of our body, and stop for a few minutes.

Then by moving our hands one at a time, we bring energy to our eyes, which allow us to look and see from the first day of our life, from birth, to the end of our days.

Let's dive into our irises of many different colours. We put our hands on our eyes and feel the energy flow towards them. Let's stop for a few seconds and then slowly put our hands on our ears.

We place our hands on our ears, we feel the energy flow, we feel the energy enter the ears; the ears that allow us to listen and hear. We thank the ears for all this.

Slowly, we bring one hand to the nape of the neck and the other to the throat. We give energy to the throat chakra in front and behind, to the vocal cords and to the thyroid.

With the hand on the nape, we focus on the occipital area and we work on the cerebellum, which helps us with muscles and voluntary movements.

Slowly, we move the hand that is at the throat and place it on the forehead to give energy to our brain, which is the home of our thoughts, of our mind, but also home to the central nervous system.

It is also the home of the glands that are found in the brain, such as the pituitary gland. Let's give love to the brain, thank the brain for the help this amazing organ gives us in our life.

Continuing to give love to the brain, we bring both hands on the head, one at a time, to flood the crown chakra and the whole brain with energy.

We give love and energy to our whole head.

From the head, we move our hands one at a time to our chest, which is the home of the heart chakra, the home of feelings. We give a lot of energy to our heart, so that it makes us feel good about ourselves and others.

The heart chakra is green so we visualize green energy and feel it pervade the whole area of the heart and chest as well as the glands located in this area, such as the thyroid, parathyroid, and the thymus.

By giving love to this part of the body, we also give energy to our lungs.

Let's move our hands now to the Solar Plexus Chakra, whose colour is yellow. This is the home of negative emotions such as anxiety, worry and discouragement but also positive ones of confidence, spontaneity, and self-acceptance. In Sanskrit, it is called *Manipura*, which translates as 'City of Jewels'. The Japanese call it 'our first brain'.

We place our hands on our body, and feel the energy flow in our organs: in the stomach, liver, pancreas, kidneys and all other organs that are found in that area.

We let our hands slide all over the body, front and back, back and forth. Now let's put our hands on the sacral chakra, which is located a few centimeters below the navel. Its colour is orange so we imagine an orange energy permeate this area; we feel our organs receive all the love they need.

We feel the colon and the organs close to the sacral chakra; we feel the proper functioning of all organs.

This chakra is the home of sexuality, communication and creativity, and it is in close connection with the throat chakra (these two chakras are the Yin and Yang of the chakras).

Finally, we run our hands over our root chakra, which is located at the base of the spine. This chakra allows us to be well rooted, or grounded, in the earth.

We give energy to our legs, which support us and enable us to walk and to run. We give energy to our feet, which bear all the weight of our body and help us move forward in life day after day.

After giving so much love to our body, we thank all our organs for the work they do that enables our life to flow in a serene and peaceful way.

We remind our organs that it is right that they send us signals from time to time to inform us that they exist and that they too need to be taken care of on a daily basis.

Of course, to do this treatment you need to take some time and not be in a hurry. By doing so, we thus realise that we are a set of parts that individually are crucial to the health and wellbeing of our whole organism. Thanks to these treatments we are better able to love ourselves and each other.

CHAPTER TEN

THREE LEVELS OF REIKI

The three levels of the Reiki natural healing method correspond to Body, Mind and Spirit.
The Reiki system I use is the Usui Shiki Ryoho, which has three levels and was founded by Mikao Usui, Chujiro Hayashi and Hawayo Takata.

REIKI LEVEL ONE
The first level teaches what Reiki is and its history from Mikao Usui onwards. Since this discipline is based on an oral tradition, the student learns the lineage of the Masters, which ensures they receive the Reiki of origin. As well, they learn about the chakras and how to balance them. They also learn how to treat themselves with Reiki.
During this level, students are given four attunements (also called initiations or activations) and are taught to primarily use Reiki on themselves, as well as family and friends.
Receiving the attunements is the process of receiving the ability to channel Reiki energy for the rest of your life. A student practitioner's subtle energy channels are opened when they receive the four attunements and by doing so they are prepared for Reiki, having activated new pathways of energy in their body.
This first level includes healing the recipient, or client, on the physical level, which is the lowest level of vibration. The student learns how to place their hands in the different positions for giving Reiki, either directly on themselves or on the client's body.

21-DAY CLEANSE

Immediately after completing the first level Reiki course, it is necessary for the student to give themselves a Reiki healing treatment every day for 21 days, this is a cleansing process and a purification of the chakras.

This treatment on yourself is very important and helps both purify the body and establish Reiki as a daily habit. It has the added benefit of increasing the flow of Reiki through your hands, as the more you use Reiki, the more you will have available to you.

Over these 21 days, every chakra is cleansed and energised and the body is purged of toxins so it is important to have a healthy lifestyle and good hygiene habits: eat well, drink a lot of water, get plenty of sleep, and try to avoid coffee, cigarettes, alcohol, etc.

During this period, you may experience small annoyances, a much more sensitive emotional state, headaches, very vivid dreams, or other feelings and sensations.

This happens because the body is being purified and is crossed by the energy for the first time. After the 21 days, any discomfort should disappear. Of course, it is important to continue treating yourself even after the 21 days but the 21-day cleansing process will ensure you are familiar and comfortable with self-treatment.

This is the most physical part of the process because the body receives healing, but it is also just the beginning of the journey.

THE CHAKRA SYSTEM

Just as there are seven days of the week, you have seven major chakras, which are located along the spine, from the root chakra at the base of the spine, to the crown chakra at the top of the head.

MONDAY Root chakra
TUESDAY Sacral chakra
WEDNESDAY Solar Plexus chakra

THURSDAY Heart chakra
FRIDAY Throat chakra
SATURDAY Third Eye chakra
SUNDAY Corona chakra

Give yourself a Reiki healing in the morning and evening. In the evenings after self-treatment, hold your hands over the chakra of the day for 15 minutes to purify and cleanse it. Later in the book, you will find a more detailed description of the self-treatment.

REIKI LEVEL TWO

The second level of Reiki training is more powerful and increases the healing energy. The attunements occur at a slightly higher vibrational level and are focused on the body's emotional, mental and spiritual planes.

In Reiki Level Two, three sacred symbols are taught to the student and attunements activate these three symbols, which are the energy keys to unlock the door to this new path; a path that leads to new knowledge. The second level Reiki is used in the same situations as the first level, but now the sacred symbols can be used to amplify the healing effect.

At second level, more of your energetic channels are opened that will enable you to feel more of the higher energies around us.

In the second level, three sacred symbols are given that have, in fact, previously been used on an unconscious level. These symbols were placed into the aura of the student as part of the Level One initiation process. The result being that the symbols are unconsciously transferred through the hands during the healing process.

After the second level attunements, the student may find that old emotions, negative mental models and past lives begin rising to the surface. They are coming to the surface in order to be completely healed, thereby helping to balance the whole being.

Mental healing at this second level means that now we are able to connect with our super-conscience and heal through our spirit, as in the case of conditions like depression, insomnia and addictions. Previous negative behaviour models can now transform to positive ones.

The second level is based on learning the first three Reiki symbols; what they are called, what they mean and how to trace them. Students also learn more about the emotional causes of disease and gain the ability to heal at a deeper mental and emotional level. Distance healing is also taught and two more attunements are given. I have chosen to make the first three symbols of this level public because in this era there is no longer any reason to keep them veiled in secrecy and available to only a chosen few.

The student Reiki practitioner will use the energy in the same way as they did after level one but now, after the second level, the student also has the ability to consciously use the sacred symbols to amplify the healing effect.

By drawing the symbols and mentally quoting them at the same time, as if they were mantras, the power of Reiki increases considerably.

The attunements for the second level also provide methods and tools for giving a Reiki session to someone who is not physically present, therefore remote healing regardless of space or time. In these cases, we talk about remote Reiki treatments, or distant healing.

How can Reiki energy be sent over distances? Because thoughts, emotions and energy travel just like electromagnetic waves from one point to another in space.

Situations, events, lives, and personal karma already experienced in the past can be cleaned up and clarified using this form of distance healing.

REIKI LEVEL THREE

Reiki Level Three is the Master level. It is the most spiritual level, and also the most challenging one to attain. It is the most spiritual and most demanding level to reach and is divided into three years of preparation. I will explain this in greater detail later in the book. During the third level, the fourth and fifth Reiki symbols are taught. The student learns the names of the symbols, their meaning, and how they are traced. Another four attunements are given. At the end of the third level, which is reached after three years, you become a Reiki Master and at this point you can teach Reiki to others.

You reach the third level with perseverance, practice, and with a great sense of responsibility.

The source of Reiki is undoubtedly Mikao Usui, who has transmitted his knowledge orally: hence the importance of the oral tradition, but also of the lineage of the therapist from whom the three levels are received.

At the third level, the therapist receives the great legacy of activating in others the ability to transmit Reiki. With the activation of the third level, the fourth symbol is received. Called Dai Ko Myo, this is a powerful and energetically superior symbol. It is used to activate the energetic channel that connects individual consciousness to universal consciousness. The fourth symbol is that of Revelation and the Light, which leads to becoming a therapist who can shed the ego self to understand themselves as part of All That Is; union with the universe. This enables the Reiki practitioner to offer their hand to others to guide them to a greater knowledge of pain and of themselves.

This fourth symbol is very powerful and is capable of bringing out the power of a person that results from union with their High Self, a state that has been forgotten over the centuries. Thanks to it, the therapist reunites with the supreme part of themselves and is ready to walk the path to enlightenment.

It is not said that the third level practitioner must reach full Realization in this life, but on receiving the fourth symbol, a person is certainly walking along the path towards achieving this goal.

The spiritual evolution leading to the fourth symbol continues throughout the therapist's life and is the source of healing. During the activation ceremonies at all levels, the fourth symbol is used by the Master to unlock and activate the energy channels of each level. The achievement of the third level takes place with deep involvement of the will and the mind but is grafted onto a burning heart and a pure soul.

The path that leads to this point is made due to determination and will but it must be accepted by the intellect and purified by the heart because it is a choice of love. The Reiki Master gives love at all times, especially when they dealing with their students.

CONNECTION TO SOURCE

The three levels of Reiki, therefore, lead back to the Body, Mind and Spirit.

Reiki is transmitted through an attunement ritual. This attunement connects the therapist to the source of Universal Energy throughout life. The connection to source and the ability to channel the energy increases most in the subsequent ritual moments.

To connect to the Universal Energy, the recipient places their hands on their own body, or the body of another person, to make the energy flow through their body automatically, as though they are a funnel.

From the first to the third level, the path to take is important: it goes from dark to light, from self to love for others.

In the first level, you abandon yourself to energy, which is intelligent and knows what the patient's needs are, but remains firm, almost passive.

In the second level the patient becomes the protagonist. They learn and use what has been learned to on themselves as well as to help others.

The third level is that of Harmony: the Reiki practitioner merges with the energy, lives on the light that spreads inside them and lets this light flow to others as a gift of love. It is very important, therefore, that the practitioner goes on a journey of deep self-healing and digs deep within.

That's why you have to be wary of the people who suggest that this third level can be done in a weekend.

In truth, it is a painful and difficult path. The third level student must go deep within themselves to uncover and uproot all the darkness, shame, guilt, sadness, etc. that the symbol of light must illuminate.

How precious it is to have the life of those who trust us in their hands! And how much attention, humility and devotion must be had to treat this priceless gift!

EXERCISES FOR THE SECOND LEVEL

EXERCISE 1 - HUI YIN CONTRACTION

During the second level, the Hui-Yin contraction technique is also learned. Pronounced 'way yin', this is a point between the anus and the genitals (the perineum) that is contracted to regulate the flow of energy. It is used with a tongue position, namely placing the tip of the tongue against the palate.

The Hua-Yin contraction should be applied by the Reiki practitioner during treatments to better conserve and circulate the Reiki energy in the body. As well, it is used by a Reiki Master during the attunements of their students.

Therefore, the channeling of energy is not only a spiritual process, it is also a physical one. A Reiki practitioner must control the breath and maintain the Hui-Yin contraction to push the energy up through the chakras, sublimating the sexual energy into spiritual energy and simultaneously closing off the root and crown chakras to keep the energy circulating in the body. The energy is thus 'blocked' and can be channeled into the hands of the practitioner.

The contraction of the Hui-Yin point must be maintained from the beginning of the treatment. The Hui-Yin contraction connects the Vessel of Conception (Yin) and the Governor Vessel (Yang) to the centre of the body, to correspond with the perineum; without it the Ki flows in the channels in opposite directions, first internally, then externally, in a rectilinear position.

If, on the other hand, the Hui-Yin is contracted, then the energy is allowed to flow in a closed circuit inside the body. This develops the propulsive force for the Microcosmic Orbit, which is a Taoist Qigong energy cultivation technique.

Without the Hua-Yin contraction, the Ki cannot be activated, nor is the Microcosmic Orbit completed. The Hui-Yin contraction allows, amongst other things, the flow of Reiki through the practitioner's body so that they can transmit the harmonisations to the students, according to the attunement technique that I have adopted.

With the Hui Yin contraction and with the activation of the Hara line (an energy line that starts three and a half feet above your head and shoots down into the core of the Earth), foreseen by the modern method, four combined attunements are established for each level. The activation of the Hara line means getting much more effective results from the Reiki session, which is something I've witnessed for myself and which has been verified by many of my students.

HOW TO DO HUA-YIN CONTRACTION

First, locate the relevant muscles located between the genitals and the anus. Then place the tip of your tongue on the palate, behind the teeth. This connects the Vessels of Conception and the Governor (also called the Central and Governing meridians).

Three tongue positions can be used for this purpose. The simplest is called the Wind and it requires only light pressure. Lightly touch the tip of your tongue on the roof of the mouth, the palate, for the duration of the exercise. This must also be done by the Reiki Master to transmit the harmonisations. Touch the upper palate with the tip of the tongue. Then, when you use the Microcosmic Orbit technique, the better it will be. If practiced regularly, then in time you will feel a sense of profound well-being and various problems of a psycho-physical nature will begin to resolve. These exercises cause the release of endorphins in the brain, providing a sense of well-being.

The Hui Yin contraction is an example of transforming sexual energy into Spiritual Energy, as well as activation and strengthening of the original Ki.

It also represents a fundamental element of Kundalini Yoga and Ch'i Kung and is widely covered in various books focused on these disciplines.

In Kundalini Yoga, this contraction of the intimate muscles is known as the root lock, or mula bandha. 'Mula' referring to the roots of a tree or plant and 'bandha' meaning lock or block. It is a technique for redirecting excess sexual energy (Kundalini energy is in fact energy of lunar, female, Yin origin) so that it can develop its potential creative and repair of the body. Thus begins the process of transforming the energy from heavy to thin.

EXERCISE 2 - SIDDHASANA

With this yoga position, or pose, we can place physical pressure on the perineum point.

You sit on the floor, on a mat, with your legs stretched forward; the left leg is folded up to bring the heel of the foot against the perineum, then the right leg is folded up to bring the right foot over the left so that the heel is pressed against the pubic bone. In this position, the spine stretches upwards, relaxing the shoulders and slightly tucking the chin.

Called siddhasana, which translates as 'perfect pose', 'accomplishment pose', or the 'pose of realisation', it is ideal for meditation aimed at spiritual growth.

If the position is a little challenging for some people to assume, then pressure can be generated by placing the heel of a foot (a cushion or other object) in contact with the perineum.

The closure of the Hui Yin (perineal point) brings Earth Ki up to the Hara line in the solar plexus, while at the same time pulling in universal energy.

When the two energies, celestial and terrestrial, meet, they generate heat, which subsequently moves towards the base of the vertebral column (coccyx and root chakra), releasing the Kundalini energy.

There are other asanas in Kundalini Yoga that allow you to exert pressure on the perineum.

The exercises that teach you to contract Hui-Yin without external pressure but simply by using the perineal musculature, are an indispensable technique for a Reiki practitioner who is called to pass the attunements to the students, standing and moving between them, as well as for transmission of the same according to the non-traditional Reiki method.

For anyone who is disabled and so unable to carry out this contraction of the intimate muscles, the guiding spirits will intervene, equally allowing a correct passage of the harmonisations.

The exercises for channeling Ki are the link between the second and third Reiki levels. Before starting to work with third level Reiki, the student must be comfortable with the symbols and be able to draw and use them for direct healing, as well as for purposes other than healing. They must also be able to perform a healing at a distance.

PURIFYING THE CHAKRAS FOR SEVEN DAYS AFTER THE SECOND LEVEL

As there are seven major chakras and seven days of the week, for the first seven days after completing the second level of Reiki, you draw a large Sei He Ki symbol on your body, which is one of the sacred symbols learnt at level two. As well, draw a Sei He Ki on the chakra of the day and then perform self-treatment.

At the end of the self-treatment, close the work by tracing a large Sei He Ki all over your body, If you have performed the self-treatment in the morning, after the Sei He Ki you can trace Cho Ku Rei on your energised chakras.

In the evening, I recommend that you trace only a large Sei He Ki before falling asleep, lulled by the Universal Energy of Reiki.

DISTANT REIKI

Distant Reiki should be sent for three consecutive days, ideally at the same time of day. It is performed by looking at a photo of the person to be treated, or by using any object (doll, pillow, stuffed animal) that can act as a surrogate for the person, especially if you do not know them.

In both cases, the therapist must have permission to send them this healing, but this can be granted psychically or via their higher self. In this case, the Reiki practitioner will be able to perceive the signal.

With permission granted, get into a meditative state and bring your focus and attention onto your distant client. Visualise the sacred third symbol in a purple light coming out from your third eye chakra and heart chakra. Imagine the symbol entering the body of your distant client through their crown chakra.

Imagine this passage of energy as a triangle, the vertices of which are represented by the three chakras involved: the third eye and heart chakras of the Reiki practitioner and the receiver's crown (see figure on next page).

The flow of energy that is sent to the distant client through their crown chakra radiates throughout their body, finding the parts to be healed.

This technique is also used in the presence of the person to be treated if it is not appropriate to touch it directly. For example, for cultural or religious reasons, when there is not enough time, or in the case of pain or risk of infection.

The person who sends Reiki distantly is also able to direct healing energy to past situations in the client's life, or in their own in the case of self-healing.

Furthermore, this type of treatment can favor the success of present and future projects. Distant Reiki can also be sent to planet Earth.

CHAPTER 11

THE SYMBOLS OF REIKI

In Hawayo Takata's time, symbols were kept secret and nobody could look at them except those who had already acquired the second level. The Master explained the symbols which, after being memorized by the students, were destroyed.

It is no longer a time for hidden teachings so I am sharing the first three sacred symbols here, however if you have not had the second Reiki level attunements, these symbols will have no value or usefulness.

In other books on Reiki, you may find the same symbols drawn differently to those in this book. Personally, I have tried to offer the simplest possible method, so that even those who are not able to draw well, will be able to draw them easily. I think it's crucial for these symbols to be understood and used. I strongly believe that Reiki will help improve our future, especially if it's widespread among young people.

There are a total of five symbols in the Usui system of Reiki. Three are given in the second Reiki level and two others are given in the third Reiki level. They are taken from Japanese kanji so they are simply words from the Japanese language. In fact, the first two symbols, Cho Ku Rei and Sei H Ki, are of shamanic derivation and are born from a combination of Sanskrit and Japanese kanji, while the third symbol of level two, Hon Sha Ze Sho Nen, and the third level Master symbol, Dai Ko Myo, are instead completely in Japanese kanji.

The symbols of the Master are also part of the Zen symbols, because Usui interacted a lot with the Buddhist monks. Reiki symbols can be activated by pronouncing them or marking them with the hand with intention, so that they can channel the energy by themselves. However, it is important to remember that they prove to be useless if the respective attunements have not been received.

During the second level Reiki seminar, the Master first tracks and then memorizes the symbols, initiating the students so that the symbols act on the mind, body and soul. From that moment on, the student Reiki practitioner will always draw on them every time they channel energy.

Reiki symbols are not drawn by all Masters in the same way. Hawayo Takata herself did not always draw them the same way.

After the death of Takata, during the assembly of Reiki Masters who gave birth to the Reiki Alliance (as reported in the testimony of Carell Ann Farmer), the Masters compared how they all drew the symbols and it was found that everyone drew them slightly differently. This was most probably a result of the veil of secrecy that had been placed over the symbols, thus preventing any standardizing of the symbols or the keeping of a written record. However, it became understood that the precision of the stroke was not important. What was important was the energy that is transmitted at the moment of attunement. The power of symbols derives from energy and brings it back to it.

Reiki is an exchange of energies. We are Energy and there will always be an energy exchange when Reiki is given and received.

The attunements at the second level provides the student with an amount of energy that allows them to make a leap in awareness further than the first.

This upgrade is given precisely by the symbols that represent the tools to move from one level of consciousness to a higher level.

By pronouncing or tracing one or more symbols, the Reiki practitioner will be able to recall all the energy of the same symbols to themself.

The symbols of the second level are:

- Cho Ku Rei
- Sei He Ki
- Hon Sha Ze Sho Nen

Cho Ku Rei is not an ideogram but derives from Tantric Buddhism and means 'by order of the Emperor' or 'by the will of God'. It is the symbol that is used to give energy, vigor and strength, because by marking it you go from the single stretch to the concentric universe.

Sei He Ki is also not an ideogram but derives from Sanskrit. It is the symbol of peace, serenity and harmony and it is the mental symbol that brings out emotions and suggestions. It is the symbol that takes us from the world of emotions to that of desires.

Hon Sha Ze Sho Nen is a set of Japanese kanji and forms a mantra. It is the symbol of distance healing and is used in all treatments that go beyond space and time because it allows the passage of energy from one consciousness to another. Distance treatment is based on this principle and allows communication between the consciousness of individuals. The symbols of the third level, however, are those that unite and overcome individual consciousness to bring it to Universal Consciousness. That is why they are taught in the level that leads to becoming a Master, as a Master is one who serves Universal Consciousness.

The second Reiki level therefore consists of a set of three sacred Sanskrit Symbols, which possess vibrations characterized by a higher spiritual implication, when used properly.

These three symbols, together with the third level Reiki symbols, are the same that Mikao Usui received on Mount Kurama during the fasting and meditation period.

When the Reiki practitioner uses the symbols in a Reiki healing, the symbols should be displayed in a violet-coloured light and at the same time drawn on the patient's body three times in a row.

Each time a different symbol is applied, different vibrations are activated. The degree of activation power depends very much on the accuracy with which the symbols are drawn.

All the symbols of the second level should be memorized and can be drawn in various ways.

For example, with the palm of the hand and the fingers together, or with the fingers spread, or using the thumb, forefinger and middle finger only, together.

Symbols are usually illustrated with directional arrows, which show how they should be drawn.

The second level attunements are necessary for the recipient to use the symbols.

The energy that activates the symbols can only be received by a Reiki practitioner, the symbols alone have no value.

People receiving second level attunements have the symbols already in their aura, as they are placed in their aura during first level Reiki attunements.

Before the symbols are drawn in second level Reiki, they are channeled with the Reiki energy through the hands.

Once the Reiki Master starts the attunement for the person who receives the teaching of the symbols and their use, the symbols then represent a sacred verbal agreement, which must not be revealed in any way.

CHO KU REI

VORTEX OF LIGHT, GROWING FORCE

This symbol in Reiki is known as the 'spiral of light' and is used to direct and focus the force.
The spiral recalls the shape of a shell and symbolizes the call to heaven.
The spiral always represents Universal Energy because it grows from the infinitely small to the infinitely large, therefore from the individual to the Universe; from the inner energy which, when released, can flow in greatness and from there go to the plane of matter.
That is why a treatment always begins and ends with Cho Ku Rei.

By displaying the Cho Ku Rei symbol, your ability to switch to Universal Energy has increased considerably.

The symbol must be drawn clockwise three times.

The syllables CHO KU REI must be pronounced mentally.

It is good to use the symbol every time you practice a Reiki session.

Cho Ku Rei acts on the physical body and gives energy.

SEI HE KI

THE SYMBOL OF HARMONY

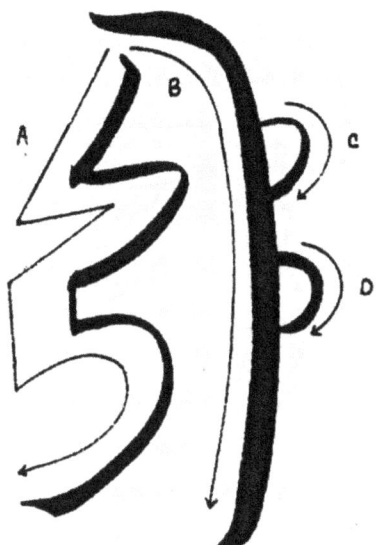

Sei He Ki is used to align the body and balance the upper four chakras on an emotional level.
If the emotions underlying trauma and ailments are not removed, they can give rise to real physical illnesses.
So the key to healing a disease, any disease, is about healing its emotional origin.
Reiki energy works to take care of this emotional aspect, clearing out the four chakras of the upper body, and flowing to where it is most needed.
Given the importance of the emotional sphere as the cause of many diseases, this symbol should be evoked in every healing as it is specifically used for emotional clearing.

The patient, thanks to this source of energy, is able to reconnect with the emotional cause of their pain long enough to be able to process it, release and overcome it.

This allows for complete recovery from the emotional pain.

The Sei He Ki symbol has a relaxing and pacifying action.

As with Cho Ku Rei, the Sei He Ki symbol must also be traced three times in the air over the client's body at the same time as the practitioner mentally repeats the name of the symbol.

Sei He Ki acts on the mental and emotional body. It can be used to purify medicines, food, the rooms of the house, and more.

HON SHA ZE SHO NEN
"The Buddha who is in me touches the Buddha who is in you"

Hon Sha Ze Sho Nen (Hon - scià - ze sciò nen) is a Japanese symbol used to send Reiki remotely and means 'the Buddha who is in me touches the Buddha who is in you'.

This symbol removes past traumas, brings about change in the present and radically transforms the future. Such changes cause a domino effect that will lead to positive results.

Hon Sha Ze Sho Nen transmits Universal Energy between space-time distances and is the most complex symbol to be traced in Reiki.
It acts on the mental body.
It represents the transcendent, an openness to the supernatural.
It brings Energy from the Universe to humanity and transforms dark fears into positive thoughts.

DAI KO MYO

This level three symbol, Dai Ko Myo, works only with those who choose love and responsibility.

The first part of Dai Ko Myo's ideogram represents a man with open arms and legs, reminiscent of the Vitruvian Man drawn by Italian polymath Leonardo Da Vinci in 1490, but it is also similar to a five-pointed star.

The symbolism that we find there recalls the union between humanity and the Divine; the encounter between matter and the supernatural, the harmony between Heaven and Earth.

The second ideogram is reminiscent of a star or sun: symbols of light and illumination.

The light that allows us to go beyond our earthly boundaries and that opens our eyes, although it is painful to do so, to look at the sky.

The third ideogram is a twosome. Sun and Moon united on the path of enlightenment. The two stars that illuminate the Earth, but which also represent the male and female, Yin and Yang.

Once the fourth symbol has been learnt and understood, the initiate at the third level of Reiki is ready to start on the path that leads them to become a therapist.

The third level is that of knowledge and draws its strength from the experience and enlightenment of Mikao Usui who had both a Christian and Buddhist background.

The Master walks along the road that Christ and the Buddha walked. But what do two spiritual experiences, so distant in time, space and culture have in common?

The link between Buddhism and Christianity is deep love for others.

Love for others that for Buddha resides in renunciation and compassion and for Christ in self-sacrifice.

Buddhism practices universal brotherhood as Christianity does on the other side of the world, and Reiki is the sum of these two spiritual experiences.

Thanks to the fourth symbol, the Reiki therapist learns to open the energy channels and to operate a karmic process on others, since their role is to help their students resolve their karma.

The therapist leads the way for the student to resolve their karma by activating the student's channels to open a spiritual path that involves their whole existence.

Hence the need for a long and thoughtful preparation at the third level because, from here on, the therapist intends to first of all deeply heal themself to mark the way for others.

The third level reveals a profound truth: everyone is already a therapist at birth, because everyone is perfect in the beginning through being created in the image of God.

Reiki does nothing but strip a person of the superstructures, or negative holograms, to reach the deep truth that leads back to where everything begins: to Love.

Dai Ko Myo has considerable strength and is very powerful. Once we have learned it, we can always use it.
It can be sent remotely together with the third symbol of the second level, Hon Sha Ze Sho Nen, to treat the recipient's heart.
Dai Ko Myo heals the soul. It is the light that invests and radiates everything it touches.
It is used during initiation rites. It is the symbol of the Master and is used for all activations as well as to purify the classroom in which Reiki is taught or practiced.
The other third level Reiki symbol is the Raku, or the Sacred Lightning.
Raku has many and varied functions, one of which is to activate the Hara line, thereby awakening the Kundalini energy and aligning it with the energies of the chakras.
It is mainly used during initiations, also called attunements, and is also used to transmit sacred fire in the energy field (aura) and in the chakras.
Its meaning, in fact, is to accumulate fire, helping to direct energy into the channels during the teachings of the third Reiki level. The channeling capabilities, therefore, are much more powerful also thanks to the results of using Dai Ko Myo and Raku.

Reiki is learned, therefore, by following the three levels, which consist of initiations and learning the techniques and symbols.

The first and second levels are mostly learned in seminars lasting two to three days, while for the third level a three-year training course in Reiki is recommended.

An attunement is given at every level. These attunements, also called initiations, are made up of activations: four on the first level, and one each on the second and third levels.

The initiations are linked to the oral tradition, which is the basis of Reiki and it is for this reason that the therapist's lineage is considered fundamental. When the lineage can be traced directly back through each master, it is certain that what is transmitted comes directly from Mikao Usui. Activation ceremonies are transmitted from therapist to therapist.

CHAPTER 12

THE TEACHING OF REIKI

I teach the third level Reiki to my students over a three-year period.
I have always believed that teaching Reiki is not a simple matter; it is a mission, a dedication that one has or does not have, and as such the practitioner who approaches this level must know what they are facing. The practitioner must know how to deal with the various problems that gradually take place during the student's life; they must know how to manage an emergency situation such as a release of great energies by the students; they must learn to manage a Reiki class, which varies based on the participants in each meeting. The basic teachings are always very similar, but the rest depends on the situations that present themselves in each class and who is in front of them.
It's nice and easy to say *'I am a Reiki Master! I took a course and now I'm a teacher.'*
A Reiki teacher must first of all be ethical, give lessons and be able to help their students at any time.
Living Reiki means first of all, living it within oneself and then in daily life; living with Reiki means knowing how to manage one's life with awareness and hospitality.
Over the years, I have curated a third level Reiki course that I call the Xantia Healing Program. It in includes not only all the techniques of Reiki Usui, Karuna Reiki TM, and Advanced Reiki Training, but many other seminars that vary from crystal therapy to channeling, to meditation.

The training course lasts three years and is divided into twelve seminars, four for each year. Every three months, in classes with a maximum of 10 students, various qualified teachers impart lessons on the disciplines to be learned.

By the end of the three years, the Master student will have been exposed to a wide range of related subjects in order to decide which of the techniques they would like to make their own and incorporate into their healing practise. Each student will be able to take the path they feel most inclined to follow.

There are people who decide that Reiki should absolutely be their way and who want to combine Reiki with a meditation practise. Then there are people who, after learning channeling, decide that, by unlocking certain energies, they will follow that path.

The important thing is to be aware of the help we, the teacher, gave to that person over that period.

CLARITY ON THE TEACHING OF REIKI

I have been asked from many quarters to shed some light on the teaching of Reiki.

Given that I do not wish to judge or express personal opinions on who teaches or how Reiki is taught, I would like to say that teaching Reiki is, above all else, a service.

The qualities of a Reiki teacher must necessarily be those of a person open to others; someone who is available, welcoming, sensitive.

I have been teaching Reiki for 20 years and have always tried to do it by putting my students first on the basis of a profound need that comes from my heart.

Many students, during the journey to become a teacher, have asked me to skip the stages and shorten their path to teaching. Sometimes they're in a hurry through enthusiasm, other times for pure haste. In the worst cases it is because other teachers 'produce' new teachers of Reiki in just one weekend.

For someone like me, with the respect I have for Reiki and its message, imagining a third level being taught in three days is an absolute contradiction.

It takes at least two or three years to become a master, to make it one's life, in addition to very precise rules and principles; a real life choice based on love for one's neighbor and the search for inner balance.

I am writing this because I feel it needs to be said. Over the years, Reiki has been misunderstood, used and abused.

Reiki is only love and as such it must be taught, perceived and absorbed in one's heart.

I am writing this to you because on this Earth so tormented by pain and war, there is a strong need for peace; true peace in hearts. That peace that must overcome fear and reign on Earth.

Please, try to learn the discipline of Reiki in a respectful way. Learn to love it and if you ever receive the gift of being able to teach it, do not look at the quantity of your students but at the quality of your teaching and that of those who will become teachers thanks to you.

TESTIMONIALS

Just as it initially felt like a losing battle for Mikao Usui, who departed the Kyoto slums with some despondence because people did not understand the importance of Reiki, for the same reasons it is reductive to talk about Reiki without going into the details of healing.

This is why I believe it is vital that Reiki is taught to young people - as already happens in many experimental schools - because children, learning meditation and universal love, could certainly excel in their studies and life.

Think about what a future world could look like when we have people who have prepared themselves for the school of life through learning techniques of relaxation, meditation, and unconditional, universal love! I am sure many will view such a vision as a utopia, but I am convinced, deep in my heart, that future generations will be able to understand that Universal Energy, through Reiki, can open the mind and heart to create a better world.

Over the years I have collected many testimonies, since I have treated so many people and born witness to their joys and sorrows.

Here are some of them.

XANTIA HEALING PROGRAM
Why the third level lasts three years...

I HAD CHANGED VIBRATIONS

"I had changed vibrations; I had decided to remove the weights. I had recently realised my infinite defects and, even more surprisingly, I had the feeling that they could turn into something magical and bright.

I decided to take all the roads that at that moment 'felt' right for me, like entrusting myself to a river even though you don't know where it will take you, but you know very well that it will cross unknown and desired places.

This is how Reiki arrived in my life: on that unknown river where I had decided to let myself go.

I had already heard of this discipline, but I had never found the desire to face this chapter, until they told me about Gaetano Vivo, a soul brother from the start.

From the first phone calls with Gaetano, I felt a great serenity in me, rarely experienced with other human beings.

I understood that I would attend his first Reiki level. I was not wrong, I had 'heard' well; after all, it could not be otherwise when searching for the truth.

The long-awaited weekend arrived, he presented himself with a cheerful look, delicate hands, fraternal smile and punctuality: the construction of the ship began which opened the doors of my awareness.

From an early age I perceived presences at my side, bubbles of colour on people, energies that moved from body to body, other ways, other worlds... and right there I understood that I was not alone. We could talk about everything without shame because there was no judgment here, a unique environment that only an experienced master could have created.

I remember my amazement in listening to Gaetano's words, while he explained what Reiki was, how it worked, describing the aura and chakras. My gaze was so lost on his lips that sometimes he stopped to ask me: 'Hey Antonio, is everything alright?'

And I burst into a laugh of joy!

I was in the right place, with the right teacher, with the right group, with the right discipline. Everything was as it should have been.

I continued to practice Reiki until I wanted to do the second level and then the third.

On the third level course, I had infinite doubts, too many to say the same 'yes' that I had at the first level.

Was I really interested in becoming a Reiki Master?

Could I really bear the responsibility of pointing the way to other people? Was I really able?

I decided to trust my heart that until then had never been wrong. I said 'yes' once again.

We started as one of the most beautiful tales: the group made up of 20 souls looking for answers, had many doubts, all shared and all sincere, and was ready to give support.

The first third level symbol arrives and a great and delicate energy at the same time envelops us in a single feeling.

A sweet cradle where we continued to experience perception.

Subsequent meetings involved looking at subjects such as tantric numerology, mediumship, crystal therapy... subjects that didn't seem part of the Reiki discipline. Despite this, we entrusted ourselves to the heart and experience of the one we had chosen as Master.

Now, after having been on the third level course for a year, I realise that none of the subjects were outside of Reiki. Now, I realise that it's all connected with discipline, with feeling, with love.

I eagerly await subsequent encounters with this magnificent journey of souls and I think I have received a precious gift that sometimes does not need words, and only silence, love and peace.

Thanks Maestro Gaetano. Thanks also to my third level group, a fertile ground for all energetic attention."

WHEN I MET REIKI
"When I first met Reiki, I had no idea what it was or that it consisted of three levels.

It was the last piece that was missing in my life, characterized by a not quite smooth and peaceful karma: a daughter lost at almost three years of age leaves an indelible mark, but what seemed the end, in reality, was a new start... and I left.

I live and work in Naples, as a kindergarten teacher.

Once again in search of my true self, of my true being, of a new awareness, and following a path towards the Universal Source, which could help me to make sense of my new life, I landed in Reiki and Gaetano Vivo.

I learned that nothing happens by chance in life.

I was looking for a Reiki course on the internet and saw an event promoted on social media: a first level Reiki course held by the Reiki Master Gaetano Vivo.

I inquire. I search on YouTube because I want to see who he is first... something, a sixth sense, which will then be very refined, tells me that it could be fine. I contact him and begin our journey, side by side: the first, then the second level enter my daily life, yes because Reiki is a *modus vivendi*, a lifestyle; everything changes for the better and I realise the importance of this completion.

My Master is absolutely in agreement with me. Indeed it is he who, anticipating my intentions, proposed the third level to me, which, however, is a longer path, lasting three years with four annual seminars.

Now one could argue about why the length of this course, when it could be achieved in less time (some people offer it over a week, others even offer it over a weekend!).

First of all, it is a path. A path that proceeds with a natural relaxation of one's soul, which begins to resume that special place, which instead everyday life relegates to the bottom of everything.

We struggle, we run, we fall, we get up, we keep running and meanwhile the place we dedicate to the Light is more or less as big as a puddle after a storm.

We forget about it and we are overwhelmed by all our so-called problems problems. Light, Universal Energy must be put first. You cannot explain many things in a week: we would do nothing but run again, as always, as every day. The course of Indian tantric numerology, that of crystal therapy and all the others that will follow (they are in fact in the first year of this three-year certification), are appropriate corollaries that enrich a cultural background that must have its own capacity, otherwise what sense would it have? I know people who have achieved the third level elsewhere and I realised that they have no idea what they are saying or doing and others who have holes in their knowledge and skills. Holes that they cannot fill because they do not have the raw material to do it: knowledge, which is transmitted in the right way by those who know how to do it. So welcome the length of this path, welcome the sweet severity, honesty and moral standing of my Reiki Master Gaetano Vivo, his accompanying the person, with appropriate time, until the end of the path. This is what the Universe wanted from me, which through its emissaries, the Angels, led me to this type of journey. Happy journey to all, namastè."

I FEEL A UNIQUE BEAUTIFUL EMOTION.
"I found myself attending the third Reiki level because someone saw qualities in me that I could not see and for this I will always thank him. The first two levels are beautiful and bring changes in life, but the third level is something indescribable. Words fail to capture the true beauty of a new awareness that grows in those who live it.
I fully agree that this training should take three years because a Master must be able to offer his student, or his client, a wide range of tools and knowledge to bring real growth.
I feel a unique beautiful emotion, when I think of the path taken so far. I am deeply grateful for all the trust that has been placed in me.
I found myself, thanks to all the love and knowledge that was given to me and to the new family in which I find myself sharing this wonderful evolutionary growth.
I started my first level in a state of strong depression. I was lost, I didn't know who I was anymore. Today I know who I am and where I want to go, because when you have a great example, you can't help but want to be a source of change for others.
Up to now, I have helped many people through Reiki and I want to continue doing more and more, because I know I am Love, Light and Peace."

CHAPTER 13

REIKI HEALS YOUR HEART

Nowadays, the demand for disciplines that are good for the body and the soul is on the rise: hence the interest in alternative diets such as veganism or raw foodism, but most of all in disciplines that foster inner growth and that involve emotions, the health of the body and mental/spiritual development.

Most modern-time diseases are caused by mental distress and confusion. Resentful thoughts and feelings are the main causes for the obstruction and restriction of the Ki flow.

Our soul is the part of us that is constantly connected to the great and boundless energy, it is the part of us that unites us with the Universe and should be listened to, because emotions may be the causes of energy blockages that make us ill.

Reiki also heals the soul. Reiki therapists are channels through whom energy is transferred to those who need it. Channeling universal energy is the most wonderful gift one can receive and share with others. Universal love, compassion, harmony and balance give us a sense of integrity.

It is very important that those who learn Reiki respect this discipline and learn to love it and – should they receive the gift of being able to teach it – do not look at the quantity of students but at the quality of the teaching, including for those who will later become Masters. The qualities a Reiki teacher needs include being open to other people, helpful, welcoming, sensitive and mindful.

Reiki for me was a choice of love for the different and very lonely child I used to be; a child who sought shelter from the outside world in food.

I used to feel that being so different to others caused other people to send me negative vibes, which entered my body through my aura as thought forms that would impact my vital strength.

Then, universal energy took me to a crossroads. I realised that I could either go on like this or I could change my life. I felt I could not help other people as things were.

I chose to love myself, I chose self-treatment and the life I have always wanted. I embraced again that lost, lonely and desperate child so I could make him feel loved and wanted and let him continue his journey.

Naturally, the more I was losing weight, the more my emotional demons were trying to bring me back to where I was. I worked hard on self-treatment and self-healing. I worked with my inner child by taking his hand and lifting him up. The more weight I lost, the greater my energy, and the more people were following me to reassess themselves like I had done.

Reiki is my passion, my way. Reiki enables me to reach parallel worlds. It enables each of us to go beyond, to get to where the human eye and its perceptions cannot reach. I became a Reiki Master in 1996 in Sedona, a beautiful town in the Arizona desert of the United States. The special energy of the red mountains that surround that area inspired me and gave me strength in ways that I've rarely experienced anywhere else in the world. Becoming a Reiki Master has transformed and enriched my life. I wanted to become a Reiki Master because I was looking for something that could give meaning to my existence.

The transformation energy directly affects our subconscious, our thoughts and our feelings. Reiki removes 'junk thoughts' forever and works over three levels of consciousness: Mind, Spirit and Body, which are strongly interlinked.

Many illnesses are associated with emotional suffering, and Reiki helps find the cause of the problem at any level: mental, physical or spiritual.

For many years, though, Reiki was viewed with suspicion by the scientific community and the Church because they did not believe in vital energy fields.

Nowadays, the view on Reiki has changing considerably: The William Rand International Centre for Reiki Training estimates that more than four million people have achieved at least one level of training, and more than 800 hospitals in the US offer free Reiki treatment to speed up recovery and relieve pain.

Moreover, large hospitals and universities have tested Reiki on humans and animals to obtain scientific data on the benefits of Reiki on post-surgical pain, chronic pain, and conditions such as Alzheimer's Disease and depression.

At the Columbian Presbyterian Medical Centre in New York, heart surgeon Mehmet Oz is famously assisted by Reiki practitioner Julie Motz during open-heart surgery.

The conclusions doctors have come to are very encouraging and offer hope for expanding the discipline throughout the country. Effects were shown on relaxation and pain relief, on the frequency, intensity and duration of migraine attacks, and on depression caused by other conditions. Studies on cancer patients show the benefits of Reiki at various stages of the disease, and in association with palliative care, as well as in relation to the ability to activate one's physical and emotional resources to cope with the disease.

This is why I think it is important to teach Reiki to young people – as is already done experimentally in many schools – because, by learning meditation and universal love, pupils can excel in their studies and in life. Think what it will be like to live in a world where people have attended a school of life that taught them relaxation and meditation techniques, as well as unconditional and universal love!

Over the years, I have gathered many testimonials from the people I've treated, here are some of them:

My Journey to the Naked Truth
"Just like the waves of the sea, Reiki has given me its movement, by getting in touch with my deeper currents, with the sand at the bottom of my rough oceans, amid shells and the tails of the storms... Reiki calmed my sea shores when they were longing for peacefulness and knowledge, and enabled all my perceptions to flow naturally, clearing my mind and making me more self-confident. Just when my hands touched the most material part of myself, and they supported it, caressed it, until they entered the circular soul, the spirals of white light that clear and heal every wound... This is Reiki to me, a caring caress, the loving thoughts we need to live, the lymph that nourishes the branch of the plant and that makes new flowers blossom... Reiki is chant, meditation and prayer flowing over the frequencies of elemental energies, vibrating deep inside each of us... reaching our most subtle parts, our border lines between the visible and the invisible, between the physical body and the essence, to bring a fragment of Light deep inside each of our single cells.
I discovered Reiki when I was going through a personal crisis, when many parts of me were upset, when my supposed self-confidence had collapsed. I was on my own, and I was 'Me'. That's when I came across Reiki, on my journey to the naked truth. The Universe is a great Mother who loves every child of hers, every smallest creature of hers. At that particular point in time, the Universe welcomed me and gave me strength, warmth and passion to continue my journey, despite my grievances, my failures and my tears. Miraculously, it turned all this

into a spiral of Light that now brightens up every part of my life, that gives me peace, whereas I used to be filled with anxiety, uncertainty, doubts, mainly due to my need to belong to material things that, being "things", sooner or later can disappear."

An Endoscope for the Soul

"I've always been intrigued – almost to the point of being nosey – by energies.
I still remember my mother's and my aunt's look when I told them I wanted to buy a book on magic. I was very young, and at that age one tends to put everything in one basket.
I really wanted Reiki to be part of my life, I bought books, I researched, but things – as we all know – happen only when the time is right. A few months ago, I took part in a free Reiki event. That's when everything became clear: the doors to a new journey were opening. I shouldn't define Reiki as a discovery, rather as recognising things, flows and situations I could not name before. A thematic focus, where the theme is the soul.
Reiki has taught me to give things their name; to give a new name to the words Love and Light, to cradle and cuddle my inner child, to set off the volcano that's inside me, to better understand myself and others. Maybe this is the greatest enrichment I owe to Reiki and, as a consequence, to my Master: being able to look beyond things, beyond people. By better understanding myself, I can better understand others, I have a new observation tool. Reiki provided me with an endoscope for the soul."

An Ongoing Embrace of Care and Love

"Reiki truly teaches us many things about life, but I think that balance is the most important of them. When we are 'balanced' with ourselves, wonderful and unexpected things happen. A few years ago, I had a

negative attitude, I would wear black clothes most of the times, I couldn't get involved in the energy of colours... I did not understand that by doing that I was expressing only closure, and I was attracting situations that did not bring any fluidity in my life, quite the opposite in fact. I wasn't well, but I barely realised it. I was too uptight and I was afraid of my emotions, I would rarely let out something about myself that wasn't my exterior appearance. Then everything slowly changed, the light began to filter, to come inside me, to bring me white clouds and sky, where there was mainly darkness. Reiki came towards me when I was ready to embrace it, and it brought about a wonderful change. It lit up all those colours I wanted to keep off, and it gave me strength, so much strength, to support myself and everything around me. There is a great intelligence inside each of us, that does what is best for us, for our wellbeing, to make us progress in our conscience. Reiki is an ongoing embrace of care and love, and we are all here to embrace ourselves."

Learned Teachings

"My quest continues. I have great trust in my quest and I really hope that one day I will be able to help every person that will ask for it. When we are on our own, it's easy to think about love, in all its facets, but things change when we go out and face the world. The strength of perseverance... of continuing to bring it to every person we meet. The learned teachings of the great masters will enable us to survive among so much hatred and falseness."

A Life Transition

"Reiki for me is a life transition, a watershed between my existence here and now and the old dormant me, always excessively focused on the past.

This transition was my awakening, my going back to myself, to my soul to my truth, to my true nature. Reiki is a rebalancing process, it means thoroughly looking for oneself, it is a profound acceptance of what we really are.
It is a pivotal journey that showed me the right way."

CHAPTER 14

DANCE OF THE CHAKRAS

The universal energy of Reiki is an encounter with the awakening soul. When this happens, you feel a wonderful driving force inside you; a vortex of light that is inviting you to look upwards.

You know that you are a body but do you know that everything that has ever existed in the whole universe vibrates inside your body? How can a body hold all of creation? Through energy, because the first cry we let out when we are born is made of energy.

Our energy is located in seven main centres of vital strength in our body. These are actual tanks called chakras.

Chakras (meaning 'wheels' in Sanskrit) are constantly spinning energy centres. Often depicted as lotus flowers, which are sacred flowers in India, the petals symbolise their opening. The seven major chakras, therefore, represent the seven main levels of connection and consciousness; they are a map of a person's direction from the moment they were born up to the highest levels of their spiritual growth.

Chakras have their own movement, a truly creative scenography that expresses itself as a vibrating dance inside our energetic body. It is a journey of warmth that reaches back to its atavistic snake-like movement, the Kundalini. It starts from our roots to reach the outermost foliage of our tree, and is finally released towards the blue sky. Although we are not always aware of it, we are constantly connected to the energy flow of this vital dance.

The first chakra is associated with survival, its colour is red, its element is the Earth. It is the energy centre corresponding to the foundation of a person, the acceptance of our physical body and the strength of our inner willpower. It's the expression of our primitive self, the search for shelter, the discovery of fire. The cave is our primary shelter, the bulwark that protects us from the world. The world immediately looked hostile to us, so we created a shelter, to survive the adversities outside. Only in the future, during our uphill journey to reach the higher chakras, will we understand what the actual challenges are, and that the real defence is only from ourselves. We have built our shelter, our primitive home, and we are beginning to think that we can express our thoughts in an artistic way, through drawings and symbols. We leave marks in the caves, we draw wild beasts, hunting scenes. We observe the outside world and start feeling the desire to possess it.

The second chakra is the sacral chakra...we realise that we are made not just of instinct but also of thought, therefore desire. We start discovering sexuality as the search for pleasure, as the revelation of self-awakening, through the discovery of senses. Therefore, the awakening of the sacral chakra releases the desire for pleasure. The need to satisfy the desires of the body leads to a deep relaxation, which is necessary in order to face any battle or competition with greater energy. The colour of the sacral chakra is orange and its element is water, it's a primal call to life. We climb up from the fight for survival to the attainment of pleasure, and we emerge in the planet of our ego, of the firm assertion of our existence, with our life experiences, with all the internal contradictions produced by our journey of discovery.
Next, we are in the third chakra, the solar plexus. Its colour is yellow, its element is fire. This is the chakra of transformation, where we establish a relationship with power. The transformation occurs when

we bring warmth and confidence to our inner power, assimilation energy to give strength and nourishment to our self.

The fourth chakra is the ascent towards the heart, where we begin to understand that we are not just a fighting tool at the mercy of life adversities, but also, and mostly, a tension in our spiritual side, because we feel the infinity we aspire to moving inside us. This is where we meet the soul, where we become aware of a divine look that goes beyond the contingent. The element of the heart is air, lightness. Its colour is pink/green, its beat is eternity.

Moving further up we encounter the fifth chakra, the throat. It's represented by the colour blue, and its element is ether. We recognise our creative expression, our voice as a powerful means of communication between our self and the outside world. We have finally freed ourselves from the world of the ego that pulls us inward, and we feel the need to declare our self to the world, to make the voice of our personality and of our desires heard.

The fifth chakra is closely associated with the second chakra, its first perception of desire and the explicit declaration of how much it intends to possess.
The dance of the chakras is a continuous, spinning movement. It follows its natural flow, its upwards spiral towards the highest places of the spirit. Human beings look ahead, they look at the horizon, they look at the sky.
There is a psychic dimension to our existence, a place that transcends the physical look of things and from which the human eye cannot observe. The place of the invisible. An 'empty' mental space that can be filled only by our perceptions, by our marvellous clairvoyance, our extraordinary ability to visualise. Clairvoyance, therefore, is our

intimate and superb possibility to transcend time and to travel with our mind to the past, to the present and, sometimes, to the future.

Now we are in the sixth chakra, the third eye or ajna chakra. Its colour is indigo and its element is Light. It is the seat of our third eye, which takes us to the psychic place of perception and allows us to better understand everything that surrounds us.

From here we move to the seventh chakra, the path to the crown. It is the centre of enlightenment, the heart and the source of consciousness. The seventh chakra is the star of the Universe, the crown. It is the place where time and space are, where there is no duality, where everything is perfection. The place where everything is turned into the superior image of Creation.
Human beings aim at the sky and reveal themselves. They are bodily and cosmic, and here they reach their highest nature, which is soaked with sky and infinity. The colour of the seventh chakra is white and its element is thought. From now on, a person's inner divinity will give rise to a more evolved humanism, and to new stages of experience and consciousness, in order to harmoniously blend with the project of love for which they were designed, conceived and created. We know that - from this celestial place onwards - people's faith can become the heart of their wonderful reunion with the stars, regardless of their religion. The dance of the chakras expands, the lotus flowers open up, the wheels of light spin in the ether. Man is his journey, Man is his eternity. If we can treasure the experience of this earthly life, everything will be a source of wisdom, and the sky will be as clear to us as a sunny summer morning.

Reiki also heals conditions that are not actual illnesses but that harass our spirit and cause us worry and anxiety.

These may be difficult relationships, arguments or distressing family situations: in this case, too, Universal Energy can help.

Remote Reiki treatment is possible solely and exclusively with the consent of those involved, whether it is applied to people or situations.

Reiki practitioners must have been attuned to the second level: they will be familiar with the symbols and know how to use them.

Reiki can be applied to past, present and future situations.

A Reiki treatment for past situations may seem pointless: how would healing a past experience change what transpired from that situation ?

Obviously, it would not change what actually happened but it can shift the emotions still attached to that past experience; it can dissolve the frustrations and the feelings that we, or the person we are treating, experienced.

Remote Reiki treatment can only be applied to our own past. Sending Reiki to the past of another person would not be ethical because people are the masters of their own destiny, no one can upset the destiny of another person.

By recalling the memory of the situation, we send Hon Sha Ze Sho Nen.

This treatment is used to forgive ourselves and others, by asking Universal Energy to heal the emotional wounds produced by the situation. We can recall events from our childhood or adolescence that blocked us, and we can also try to better remember them.

Remote treatment is different from distant treatment in the present. Although practitioners can remotely treat people who have expressly asked them to, sometimes they are asked for general help or they see someone suffering; this is when Reiki treatment can be suggested, after explaining how it works to those who are not familiar with it.

Reiki practitioners must ask for the client's consent because they must approach them in a humble and respectful way, and be sensitive towards those who suffer. Moreover, other people's free will should always be respected, even though it is important to also instill hope through the message of Love that Reiki brings.

CHAKRA POSITIONS

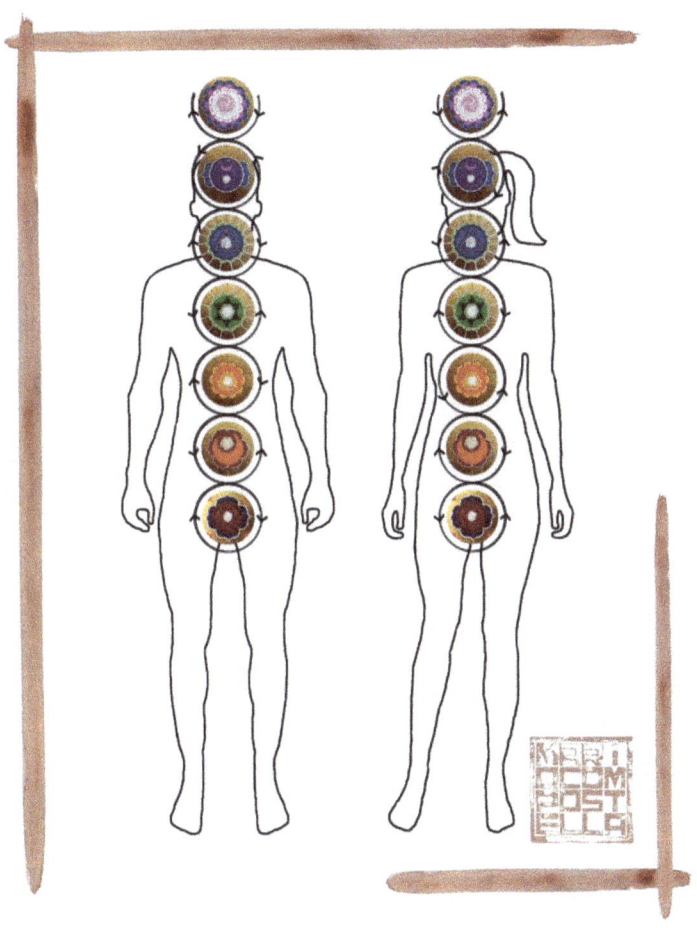

Panta Reiki — Dance of the chakras

Chakra positions and rotation in men

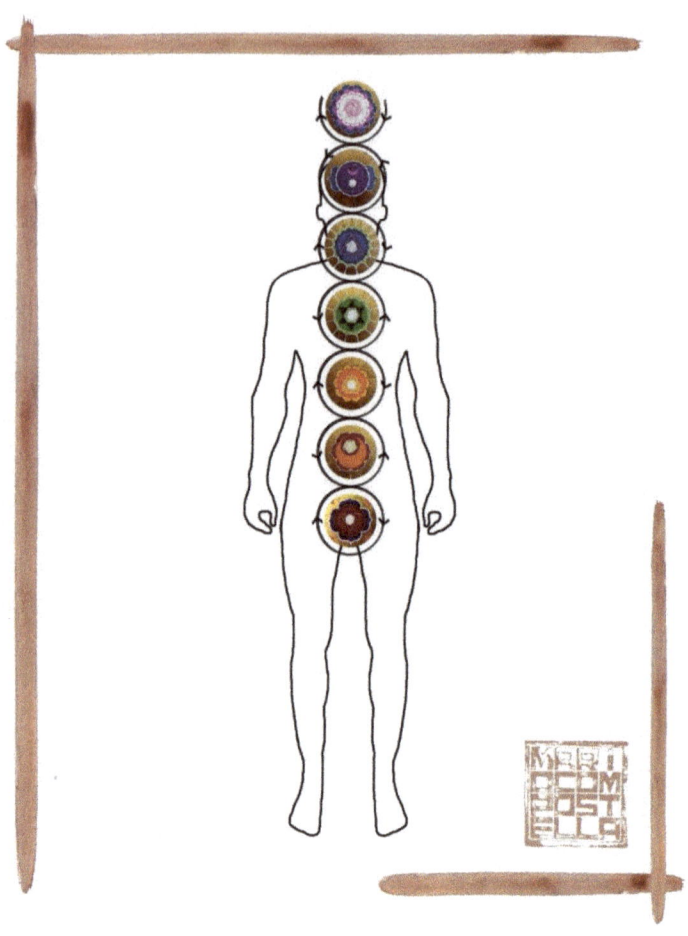

CHAKRA POSITIONS AND ROTATION IN WOMEN

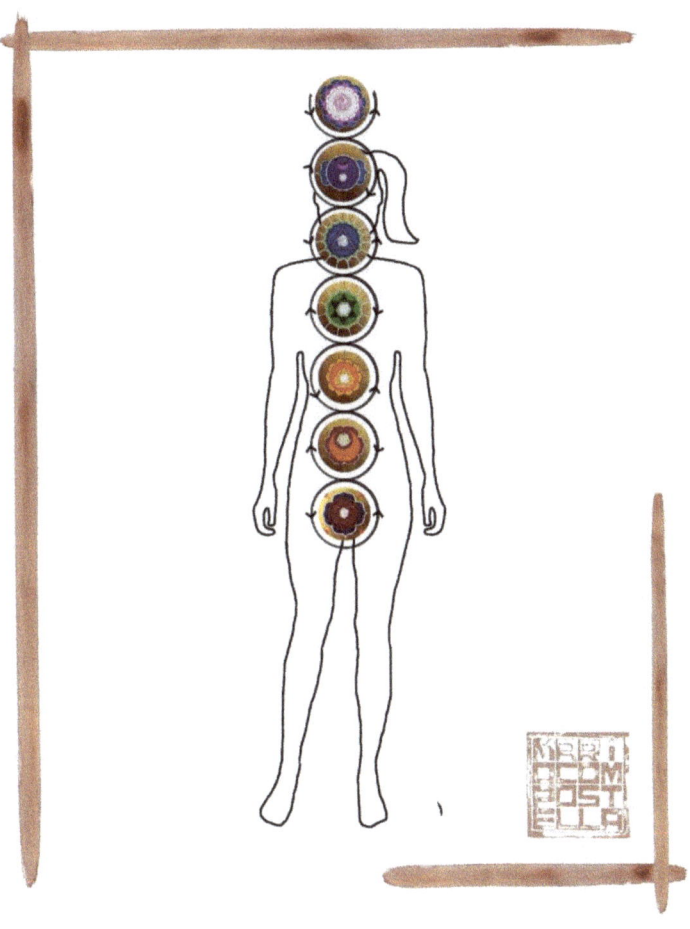

We have seen that on the first level of Reiki, the energy channels are activated by the therapist, so that Universal Energy can flow freely through the student and eliminate emotional and physical blockages. The energy centres are mainly the chakras.

CHAPTER 15

SEVEN MAJOR CHAKRAS

I ° CHAKRA - THE ROOT OR BASE

This chakra is positioned at the base of the spine. Red in colour, it represents our foundational energy; our root. This chakra deal with the need and instinct for survival, roots, stability, inner strength to face life's challenges. The root chakra enables us to look at the world with our practical sense of existing. It is the deepest connection between our physical body and Earth; its balance is important to ensure that all higher energies can flow smoothly and harmoniously, thus instilling a sense of constant trust and security.

II ° CHAKRA - SACRAL

The sacral chakra is positioned in the pelvic area.

It is the chakra of desire, of relationships with others and of emotions. From the survival instinct of the first chakra, here we begin to desire to fully live the experience of life.

The sacral chakra represents the transition from solid, radical, basic elements, to liquidity, to water: from survival to the generation of life.

It is not for nothing that the sacral chakra is associated with the moon and it is here that the ancestral energy of Earth (mother energy) meets the sky (creative energy) in an embrace of shining orange light.

It is orange light energy that caresses our aura with infinite sweetness. Energy that expands to reach new nuclei of knowledge. It is magnetic perception of desire. We carry within us visions of Love and everything is revealed in the magnificence of being.

Like flowers of harmony, each of our petals is an integrated note to another, a sound, a music that produces magnificent chords.

Orange energy supports us, rebalances our processes of evolution in the world. It is spiritual energy that includes everything.

III ° CHAKRA - SOLAR PLEXUS

It is the chakra of the shining energy of the sun that feeds everything. Love, love, love in everything we live is the yellow energy of the sun's call and transformation. The third solar plexus chakra is a place of amplification of our power, of the ego, into something higher.

This offers us the opportunity to evolve into a wider vision of ourselves. It is here that the will to act is manifested, but also the expansion of our borders and the possibility of our growth in the external world.

The solar plexus chakra is also called 'City of Light', the keys to enter it and to live in a solar and luminous way every day, in us, removing internal and external struggles and conflicts, which can prevent the extraordinary vision of a life of harmony and full beauty. Love is constantly in us, it never abandons us, it is a powerful force, a force from above. Let's find it in our smile, in our enthusiasm. Every day, a new ray of sunshine to discover, from which to be illuminated in wonderful situations of light. Life is extraordinary, with its movements, with its continuous excellent dynamics.

The first three chakras, through their development and harmonisation, help us shape a strong personality and presence, but it is above all here, in the solar plexus, that we face the tests that require courage. The courage to affirm ourselves in the world, to defend our borders, and fight for our ideals. It is the ego that affirms itself. That's fine, as long as we also learn to balance the ego's desire for expansion, to avoid the excesses of competition, to ensure that our battles are not of rivalry but of opportunity, growth and conquest of the talents that each of us of course it owns. The third chakra of the solar plexus, called *Manipura* in Sanskrit, which means 'shining gem'. It is the inner power of fire and transformation, a radiant power, shining like the sun. It is the manifestation of personality, the centre of the ego, sometimes dominant: it is very important that this energy centre is constantly balanced. Its element is fire and the colour yellow, a colour that we can see as the apex of a flame at the base of which is the red colour of the first chakra, then the orange of the second and finally the third chakra, a spark of enthusiasm leading to action. The corresponding organs are the digestive system, stomach, pancreas, liver, bile.

IV ° CHAKRA - HEART

There is no way or path that does not lead us here!
Everything starts from the heart and everything returns to the heart, in an energy flow that repeats itself endlessly.
Have faith in yourself, this is the impulse of the heart!
Here is our true centre, the seat of our soul.
Living in the heart means listening to our emotions from their deepest voice, welcoming our essence in its natural and pure sound. The heart knows everything about us and the world: it knows how to love, it knows how to forgive and then it knows how to love again.
It is a divine vibration in our humanity, the wonderful pulsation of all Existence, the source of all creation: Love.
Its Sanskrit name is *Anahata* and its colour is green. It is the place between heaven and earth: the infinite space of the Soul.
Living in the heart is no small matter, it is an act of faith, a vision of life in abundance, in the magnetic attraction of the pure elements of being.
The awakened heart is one of the greatest and simplest truths in life: the more we love, the more we will attract love experiences into our lives.
It is in the heart that we begin to experience unity with whole life. Our gaze here is already turned to the three higher chakras, looking towards the crown at the top; the magnificent energy of the universe which purifies and pervades everything, and which in the heart manifests all the extraordinary power of all its excellent vibrations.
The corresponding organs are the heart and circulatory system, lungs and liver, but also arms and hands.
The heart is the energy centre of love and balance; love as an irradiating quality that leads to harmony and which represents the overcoming of our egoic limitations and moving towards a harmonious fusion with the surrounding world.

V ° CHAKRA - THROAT

The fifth chakra located at the throat is a light blue colour. It is the first of the three upper chakras, the place where we learn to perceive and understand the collective nature of everything.

In the throat chakra, the individual perspective and the collective mind are integrated into a volcano of creative thoughts. This is the chakra of ideas, of thoughts transformed into actions, of revealed words, of art expressed in the fullness of the self. Finding your own voice is the instinct of the fifth chakra, which is not only the physical voice, but above all the place within us from which we speak. Creativity is at the highest level of the mind so writing, dance, painting... all the arts thus become our highest expression of freedom and beauty. The throat chakra is the voice of creative expression. With the opening of the throat chakra one experiences a reviving of energy. It is the pure place of creativity, of inspiration, of the expression of our personal truth and of the unique talents that each of us holds within themself.

Loving each other, knowing each other is the instinct of the fifth chakra, our word is the means to reach the outside world in the communication of our thoughts. Always take care of your uniqueness and always carry the charm of your inspiration with you. The Sanskrit name is *Vishuddha* (meaning purification) and its element is ether. The corresponding organs are thyroid, lungs, neck, shoulders, teeth. This energy centre is governed by sound. It's invisible but extremely powerful force represents the essence of communication and creativity. It is a more universal language than verbal, a channel of spiritual information beyond time and space, already oriented towards the higher planes of the higher energies.

VI ° CHAKRA - THIRD EYE

The sixth chakra is located in the centre of the forehead, slightly higher than the eyes, between the eyebrows. It is the third eye, an eye not physical but of the spirit. It is the seat of divine intuition, the feeling of being on the right path. It is the sixth sense that helps us perceive the energies that surround us and to discern what we need for our spiritual growth.

Let us pray that our journey will lead us to a subtle and refined perception of the world around us, so that nothing can disturb our purified awareness. The third eye level of consciousness is the astral brain, the emotional guide to the realm of intuition. Imagination and inspiration are our primary impulse here. Desire for transcendence, the ability to see deeply, an inner guide that derives from being aligned with a bigger reality.

The sixth chakra leads us to a place beyond the limited reality of the senses. It is the 'state of consciousness of union' in which everything appears in the form of many manifestations of the One Great Spirit.

Its Sanskrit name is Ajna, which means 'to perceive'. It is placed almost at the height of the midpoint between the two eyes. Its element is light and its colour is an indigo, a combination of purple and blue. The gland associated with the third eye chakra is the pituitary gland. The third eye also corresponds with our ears, eyes, nose and mouth as they provide the ability to hear, see, smell and taste. The third eye is our psychic tool that allows us to have a better understanding of things. Ajna is the energetic centre of the physical sight but also of the vision of the invisible, the place where the human meets the spirit.

VII ° CHAKRA - CROWN

The crown chakra represents pure and uniform cosmic energy.

The impulse of the crown chakra is to surrender to spirituality, the desire to experience the Divine, in whatever way it is defined.

The planetary soul is the essence of the world and at this level of our consciousness we feel the desire to be One with the Whole; to recognize ourselves in the collective image of the cosmic energies that constantly vibrate in every event of creation.

Meditation, prayer and deep contemplation ensure that our battles are not of rivalry but of opportunity, growth and of mastering the talents that each of us naturally possesses.

Its Sanskrit name is Sahasrara, which translates as the 'circle of a thousand rays or a thousand petals'. However it also translates as 'a thousand times as much, a thousand'.

Its corresponding gland is the pineal while the organs ruled by the crown chakra are the eyes and the brain.

The element of this chakra is thought and the colour is white. Sahasrara represents the connection between the natural universe and the spiritual universe; the connection between individual consciousness and cosmic consciousness.

The crown chakra, therefore, allows the opening of the magnificent lotus flower that is inside each of us.

THE MANTRA OF THE CHAKRAS

7. HAOM
6. OM
5. HAM
4. YAM
3. RAM
2. VAM
1. LAM

To cleanse the chakras, some powerful forms of meditation are effective, leaving the body energised and lightened of heavy energies.
Before beginning a Reiki treatment, one of the most important processes is to open and cleanse the chakras to rebalance the flow of energy.
A pendulum sensitive to subtle vibrations can also be used to locate blocked chakras. Holding your pendulum about four to six inches up the chain or string, hold the pendulum over each chakra and see if it begins to move in a strong, steady circular motion. If the pendulum does not move, or only moves in a small, weak circle, it indicates some blockage in the chakra.

CHAPTER 16

REIKI HEALS YOUR BODY

This chapter is written by General Practitioner and Reiki therapist, Dr Giuseppe Colomasi.

The role played by medical science in solving many human problems related to pain and disease is evident to all.
It has changed the world through unimaginable achievements in all fields: genetics, biochemistry, physiology, surgical techniques, imaging techniques, laboratory, pharmacology, therapy and prophylaxis.
All this has helped to give better diagnoses; to make therapies more effective and more targeted; to decrease the incidence of side effects, and to mitigate and / or modulate suffering.
It is clear that the current globalized society is crossed by profound contradictions: on the one hand we have greater well-being even if not equally distributed, but on the other hand we have epidemics of loneliness and the rise of myriad mental problems and psychosomatic disorders, which are often accompanied by the misuse of drugs, alcohol and tobacco.

PSYCHE AND SOMA

Medical science, in the wake of the results obtained and aware of its potential, tends to take an uncompromising attitude, excluding interference in its field of action. In addition, having become so absorbed by technology, it has increasingly reduced dialogue with patients, focusing on mere organicity and moving away from the dynamic interaction between psyche and soma.

Therefore, the need arises to restore the relationship between psyche and soma, focusing on homeostasis.

Homeostasis is the ability of a cell, a set of cells, (a tissue), a set of tissues (an organism), to maintain its characteristics in a balanced state. Disease manifests through a loss of homeostasis, a subjective and objective presence of a change in the body and psychic state. Disease is, therefore, a dynamic and complex phenomenon.

What matters are the infinite nuances of the experience of disease and pain: we cannot look at patients with the same disease as a homogeneous population. In other words, all the people who have a condition such a fibromyalgia do not have the same set of circumstances or experiences that resulted in this condition. The reasons one person could not maintain homeostasis are different to the reasons another person could not maintain their homeostasis.

The same can be said of the perception of pain, where subjectivity reaches almost opposite ends. The source of one person's agony is barely felt by another person.

Time is also an equally important component. There should be time to devote to each patient; time to visit them, to carry out clinical tests, to arrive at a specific and targeted diagnosis and relative therapy, to quantify a prognosis, to declare a healing, or a chronic condition. There should be time to assert that everything possible has been done and that one has to now turn to ancillary and palliative therapies. There must also be time, though, to devote to the psyche, going beyond the protocol-set way of reasoning and acting, which is certainly necessary and right, but which sacrifices the psyche, recognizing value only to the body and little to the mind.

Hence the need of the human being to seek and find crutches and handholds, which often, in a reductive and superficial way, medical science labels as complementary and alternative medicines.

After more than 40 years of orthodox practice of medical science, I had the opportunity and curiosity to approach Reiki, a method born in the East that exploits the real or considered energy fields and postulates the existence of a flow of energies vital.

Reiki is basically a relaxation technique, which if well conducted and well received, can become an ideal partner of medical science for the following reasons:

It is non-invasive (there is almost no contact between the operator and the recipient),

It is simple, it is personal, it is holistic,

It is an interior experience that captures the reality of the moment in which we are living and does it in full awareness,

We can practice it on ourselves and others, so it facilitates sharing and self-empowerment.

HOMEOSTASIS

For all this, Reiki can help restore altered homeostasis, acting on the functional component and facilitating, modifying, adapting, leveling the dynamic relationship between psyche and soma.

As an example, I have chosen the clinical case of a 54-year-old patient who has been fighting for more than 10 years with a malignant tumour of the breast. She has undergone surgery, chemotherapy, and radiotherapy. She has had a first and second recurrence of the disease and is currently undergoing experimental chemotherapy that has significant unpleasant side effects.

She told me that before practicing Reiki regularly, she had felt like a number, a medical record, a sick body. She had lost her self-confidence and no longer wanted to fight.

While medical science is working, Reiki has improved this woman's adherence to therapies; boosted her endurance to the inevitable discomforts and has given her hope, and helped bring back the smile that she had forgotten.

My teacher of pathological anatomy always asked, during master classes, exams, and whenever possible, a simple question: "Do you know what the future holds for medical science?"

Our student response was and always had to be: no!

Nobody can predict this. It will surely be a demanding, fascinating but difficult journey. A journey that does not include one destination, but many destinations. A journey that does not overcome one obstacle, but many obstacles. A journey that should be done in good company, with an ideal partner like Reiki, because the journey must never end, only travelers end.

Take this passage from the Phaedo (118 BC), a dialogue written by the ancient Greek philosopher Plato that claims to recount the events and conversations that occurred on the day that Plato's teacher, Socrates (469-399 BC), was sentenced to death by hemlock poisoning by the state of Athens.

In Plato's dialogue, Socrates' last words were: 'Crito, we owe a rooster to Aesculapius, will you remember to pay the debt?'

'The debt will be paid,' replied Crito,

Asclepius was the god of medicine and healing, and the sacrifice of a rooster was a normal offering of thanks for recovery from illness.

Does the therapist still owe a debt? The question remained unanswered.

CHAPTER 17

REIKI AND ONCOLOGY

This chapter on Reiki and oncology was written by psycho-oncologists Dr. Guendalina Di Fede and Dr. Giusy Canonico.

Cancer is one of the most common causes of suffering in the world and breast cancer is the most frequent cancer of women. In 2018, about 2.1 million breast cancer cases were diagnosed worldwide.
In the 28 nations comprising the European Union, there were 404,920 new cases with 98,755 deaths from breast cancer in 2018.
A woman suffering from a tumour pathology is projected into a complex world where there are no words, examples or gestures, where randomness, suffering, expectations and memory influence each other, intertwine, overlap until they become a tragic representation of life itself.
Even today, the diagnosis of cancer is perceived as a death sentence and initial shock is generally followed by disbelief, anger, anxiety, insomnia and depression.
Most of the people diagnosed with this condition will only partially remember the information that was provided to them. Time and space are never enough to elaborate and understand the disease and to deal physically and psychologically with the treatment.
Progress in some revolutionary and rapid treatment of tumors is helping many people to survive this disease and by the year 2040 almost a doubling of the number of survivors is expected. In addition,

a 30 per cent increase in people living at least five years after diagnosis is expected for the next decade.

Diagnosis and treatment have always had a relationship that is not always easy and is sometimes almost conflicting.

The patient must face treatment paths that are increasingly difficult and painful. These medical treatments are, unfortunately, not always effective. Despite the intense commitment of science to look for new ways to fight tumours, there is not as much attention to identify, understand or alleviate any long-term effects of therapies.

Such long-term effects include pain, intestinal ailments, amenorrhea (missed periods), early menopause, osteoarticular pain, early osteoporosis, menopausal disorders, urogenital disorders, limb paraesthesia (burning or prickling sensations), endocrine and cardiovascular disorders, increasingly frequent periods of depression, and loss of libido. Such side effects can severely reduce life quality. In this way, the complications of drugs and treatments are like a double truth.

Considering the complexity of the disease as well as the physical and psychological discomfort induced by the treatments, the cure cannot be focused only on the body. There is an increasing consensus on the importance of considering the psychosocial characteristics for cancer patients.

Attention to the person's well-being the quality of life during and after an oncological therapy have become a priority.

THE HEALING PATH

Despite the plethora of pharmacological and medical interventions, an approach that does not involve drugs can play an important role in healing. And with results ranging from 20 to 100 per cent success, it could be argued that they should be involved.

Alternative therapies, also known as complementary medicine, are becoming increasingly popular supportive therapies and are used in conjunction with conventional treatments for stress, pain and suffering, thus improving the response rate.

Reiki is a discipline of alternative and complementary, non-invasive medicine that is administered through the hands.

As already mentioned, Reiki means 'universal life energy' and at the basis of Reiki culture is the vision that every living organism, in addition to the evident physical state, is composed of energy.

This energy moves throughout the body and generates huge amounts of information in the form of energy fields. Reiki attempts to balance and strengthen the flow of this energy by stimulating the body's healing abilities.

A Reiki treatment can change a person's attitude towards the disease thus improving life expectancy by increasing the patient's willingness and ability to follow the doctor's instructions and adherence to the treatment protocols. Reiki can cause feelings of deep relaxation, of heat or drowsiness and greater well-being.

Published data on the efficacy of Reiki as a complementary therapy in the treatment of breast cancer is lacking. There are many reports but few are the well-designed studies that demonstrate the effectiveness of Reiki.

In a small Canadian study published in 1997, 20 pain sufferers, some of whom had cancer, had been treated by certified Reiki therapists to determine whether Reiki could be a useful support for conventional treatment. The evaluation of the pain scale, immediately after the Reiki treatment, showed a significant improvement. However, the results are difficult to interpret due to both the small number of patients in the study and the lack of a comparison group.

Another study found that Reiki treatment improves the quality of life of cancer patients, but did not reduce the amount of pain relief medication used. In a 2015 study by the University of California Santa Cruz, the healing capacity of Reiki treatment on cancer cells in vitro was examined. The effects on cancer cells were determined by the effects on cell proliferation, by the number of cells that enter the cell cycle and by the increase in apoptosis (death of cells). The cell lines being treated showed less proliferation, a reduction in cell cycle entry and greater apoptosis. According to the American Medical Association (AMA), more than two-thirds of the patients surveyed, who were undergoing Reiki treatment, reported a clinical benefit. As well, 84 per cent of hospitals responded positively to patients' request for complementary and alternative medicine services, such as Reiki, alongside their conventional treatment.

If we want maximum benefits from therapies and if we want both longevity and quality of life, we must look beyond the parameters of conventional medicine.

General practitioners, specialists, researchers and anyone who has contact with such a complex disease as breast cancer should recognize that taking care of the person, not just the tumour, really means making a difference in the lives of millions of cancer survivors.

Quantity, or living longer, without quality is a half life.

REIKI IN PINK

The Pink Reiki Network project is an initiative conceived in April 2018, during a round table at the Ferula Holistic Festival of Ferla, where the needs of women being operated on for breast cancer and having oncological treatment were discussed.

A cancer in the breast, due to its physiological characteristic, is a tumour that affects not only the body but also the 'Being Woman'. That is, the balance that exists between the body and the psyche. The breast is an integral part of the female body, it represents a woman's femininity and is linked to motherhood in the act of breastfeeding.

The female identity as an integral part of the body scheme and as an object of seduction. A scar in such an important and complex part of a woman's body is a scar that reaches deep into her soul and risks damaging the core of her being'. The psychological pain experienced through the ordeal of breast cancer is a pain that cannot be underestimated as it is a fundamental parameter in the quality of life and in the path of integration between body and mind.

Conventional medical treatment involves the surgical removal of the area affected by the disease in conjunction with adjuvant oncological treatments such as chemotherapy, hormone therapy and radiotherapy.

The path of treatment becomes a painful path. Suddenly, a woman's life revolves around the cancer and her existence is now dominated by appointments with doctors and by managing the side effects of the treatments. Everyday life changes, social and family relationships change, projects change and how she perceives herself as a woman changes. The breast cancer patient enters a vortex in which she loses the power to manage her life; she loses herself. It seems that it is no longer she who holds the reins of her life but instead it is now the doctors and the medical interventions that manage her life. There is a breakdown between the body and the mind.

Considering that, due to the complexity of the disease, the soma and the psyche are affected, the cure cannot be focused only on the body, but must also include a psycho-oncological path where you have the opportunity to work on the psychological, spiritual and social.

From various scientific observations it has been seen how Reiki can be a relaxing treatment, which facilitates the achievement of psycho-physical well-being, reducing the side effects of adjuvant conventional treatments.

The Pink Reiki Network project is the result of teamwork between professional and voluntary reiki operators, trained by the international Reiki Vivo school, the medical team of the Santa Lucia Nursing Home and the volunteers of the Sicilia Donna Association.

The path involves the psycho-oncologist becoming involved with the woman's recovery and rehabilitation in the phase following the surgery.

With a focus on emotional distress, the psycho-oncologist identifies the woman's primary needs, any personal and relational problems, and the possible deterioration of the quality of life caused by the oncological disease. In doing so, they identify those patients who could benefit from Reiki treatments.

As soon as the Reiki treatments have started, the psycho-oncologist guides the patient through the process of adapting to the oncological treatment path. During Reiki treatments, the woman enters a state of deep relaxation; her emotional blocks will be dissolved thanks to the combined work of the various professionals.

During the first year of the project, 25 women (a total of 250 treatments overall) participated in the Pink Reiki Network Project. At time of writing, five of the women left early; four dropped out halfway through for personal reasons, 10 are still being treated and six have completed the path. The treatment was administered weekly, or fortnightly, or monthly according to the person's needs, for a duration of 30 minutes for each treatment. All participants were given the M.S.P. Test to measure stress levels and to observe the result at the end of the treatments. The test was administered in test-rest mode, taking into consideration the M.S.P. of entry and the M.S.P. of exit.

The sample analyzed from the beginning to the end of the Reiki path consisted of six women. The two tests, administered nine months apart, have been linked and it has been shown that three out of six women experienced lower general stress levels in the re-test. In particular, the "hyperactivity and behavioral acceleration" cluster seems to be the area that derives the greatest benefit, the remaining three women did not register a significant change.

During the psycho-oncological interviews, the five women who abandoned the initial treatment, said they were unable to relax and perceive the benefits of Reiki, while the 10 women still in treatment and the six who finished the course said they experienced a decrease in anxiety, relaxation, an improvement in mood, and better quality of sleep. Beneficial aspects were recorded within 48 hours after treatment.

The integrated path between psycho-oncological support and Reiki treatment has allowed women in undergoing cancer treatment to facilitate the process of processing the traumatic event.

The women were helped to adjust to the oncological treatment period; to better manage the side effects of treatment, and to once again feel connected with their body, thus facilitating a path of integration between body and mind and the consequent quality of life improvement.

THE TOUCHSTONE PROCESS

In America since 2005, William Lee Rand, the founder and President of the International Reiki Training Centre, has developed what is now known as The Touchstone Process.

The Touchstone Process was developed as an ongoing critical evaluation of Reiki studies published in peer-reviewed scientific literature.

Basically, many studies have and are being done on Reiki but not all of them stand up to scientific scrutiny. Rand aimed to gather the most significant scientific research regarding Reiki, and make it available for general public.

So the Touchstone Process is a review method for analyzing studies carried out on Reiki programs in hospitals and clinics in the United States.

The process is rigorous, impartial and consistent and incorporates best practices for scientific review.

Rand started formulating the Touchstone Process after the development of Reiki in hospitals and it is one of a kind. There have never been so many noteworthy studies on Reiki collected, analyzed and evaluated within a single source.

According to The Touchstone Process, among the diseases and ailments that have proven suitable for the treatment of Reiki, the following can be highlighted: post-operative dental pain; the ailments of the elderly with Alzheimer's; pre-operative relaxation and post-operative pain; pain in chronic patients; depression, and stress.

As of 2009, the Touchstone Process has evaluated 25 test studies that have appeared in peer-reviewed journals. Studies reported that 83 per cent of tests showed moderate and strong evidence supporting Reiki as a therapeutic healing modality.

The Presbyterian Hospital of New York / Columbia University Campus was one of the first hospitals to offer Reiki as part of its integrative medicine (CIMP) program. One of the hospital's famous cardiovascular surgeons, Dr Mehmet Oz, brought extraordinary attention to Reiki when he invited Reiki therapists to treat patients prior to his heart operations and heart transplant operations.

Reiki was also particularly effective in cancer patients, not only as a psychological support for anxiety, fear and depression, which arise after diagnosis, but also to alleviate the side effects of chemo and radiation therapy.

In the numerous forums and blogs on the internet, you can find many direct testimonies of the experience of the patients who have tried Reiki.

Patients claim to be self-treated during therapies that require long stays.

Therefore, universities and scientific research are also playing a big part. The thesis of Dr Riccardo Monezi was published by the Federal University of Sao Paulo - Paulista School of Medicine, and was also awarded the Reiki Hayashi Research Award on the treatment of stress syndrome in the elderly.

In one eight-week study, researchers took two groups of elderly volunteers. One group received Reiki and the other group received placebo treatment. The results suggested that the Reiki-treated group had reduced levels of stress, anxiety and depression, reduced muscle tension, a better quality of life, and warmer peripheral skin temperature.

There are also countless studies such as that of Dr Natalie Trent of Harvard University, in collaboration with William Rand's International Reiki Research Centre, which aims to analyze five to six thousand cases.

There are many health centres that include Reiki treatments in therapy protocols, such as the Memorial Sloan-kettering Cancer Centre in New York, where there are six doctors and 25 nurses who practice Reiki, or at the Rhode Island State Nurse's Association, where nurses are given Reiki training.

At California Pacific Medical Centre, one of California's largest hospitals, patients who react well to Reiki treatments are asked to take a Reiki course in order to continue self-treatment, freeing the hospital's internal staff to better treat other patients.

In America, there is no mandatory register for Reiki programs but an ever-changing number of hospitals is offering Reiki services.

These prominent academic medical centres include the aforementioned Memorial Sloan Kettering Cancer Centre, NY Presbyterian Hospital - Columbia, Yale New Haven Hospital, Dana Faber - Harvard Cancer Centre, the University of Pennsylvania's Abramson Cancer Centre, Johns Hopkins Hospital and Health System, George Washington University Hospital, MD Anderson Cancer Centre, California Pacific Medical Centre.

Some hospitals, as already mentioned, offer Reiki training to staff and sometimes even community courses.

Hospitals that offer Reiki treatments bring Reiki to itself a mainstream visibility that gives credibility to a practice that is often misunderstood and underestimated.

Not everything, however, is roses and flowers, often Reiki practitioners are not integrated into health programs and can only work as volunteers. Moreover, programs are tied to funds that are not fixed.

In the rest of the world there are edifying experiences in Brazil, Portugal and Switzerland.

A nice experience is that of AICS - Italian Association of Culture and Sports - which provides practitioners from the Department of holistic sciences and techniques to train the nurses of the Sarem Women's Hospital in Tehran, a famous centre for gynecology and fertility in Iran, in the practice of Reiki, so as to integrate classic medical methods with a holistic approach.

CHAPTER 18

REIKI HEALS YOUR MIND

In 1971, yogi and spiritual teacher Gopi Krishna said the following: *"Every time I direct my mind of mental knowledge to my inner being, I invariably perceive a luminous light inside and outside my head, in a constant and continuous vibration as if a brilliant and very subtle substance climbs the spine and extends inside and out of the skull, filling and surrounding it with intense but indefinite radiation."*

Our consciousness is energy. Our spiritual body contains the blueprint of our physical body; our ethereal dimension is imbued with omniscient matter. Many years ago it was believed that the Universe was a remote place full of empty spaces. Today it is known that the universe is made up of gas and nebulae and that it is, above all, full of energy. And teeming with life. The universe itself is life. In constant progressive evolution, it is the manifestation of a supreme intelligence, of a cosmos whose extension is infinite, full of will, awareness and imagination.

"The only way we can live is to grow. The only way we can grow is to change. The only way we can change is to learn."
Gopi Krishna

In our mind, there is a place of memory where an unconscious root level is inherent and where all our experiences are stored. A root in which all the events of our lives are recorded, our cellular history, where we can find traces of our past, present and future lives. As in a timeless ego, the residue of our experiences dwell here. The mind is therefore an extraordinary archive of images provided by our own experiences, from which we draw ease or unease, depending on our projections. When our mind, our thought, wanders in the territories of the unconscious, what can rise to the surface is not always predictable.

Situations or traumas from the past that we believed resolved or that we had removed, or situations of well-being which we cannot enjoy, can re-emerge.

The measure between the opposite polarities of these two different projections is largely conveyed, as always, by our emotions. Our psyche is therefore closely related to our perceptions. Our self-perception in a given instant determines the size of our ego.

Reiki is a discipline and a technique for energy rebalancing, it is not a philosophy or a religion.

It is a practice of ancient wisdom, of luminary wisdom, which allows one to channel the energy of the universe and to transmit it to our body and mind, to restore balance in our energy flow and remove any stagnations that hinder its free flow, thus activating the body's natural self-healing capacity.

Our energy field, and therefore our entire system, and our reality, have the natural tendency to balance, reinforce or generate themselves by tending to their best.

These are the qualities of self-healing that persist in every organism (demonstrated by the fact that a wound heals by itself). Cells are subject not only to bio-physical but also bio-chemical reactions. And our mind, connected by a thin thread to our emotions, is no exception.

Since Reiki acts on the subtle and deep planes, it also brings support to our psycho-emotional level.

Today in some Italian hospitals there are already departments of integration between energy medicine, understood as holistic therapy, and traditional, academic medicine, which are integrated for a common noble goal.

Reiki acts in our physical and ethereal body through the chakras, or 'wheels', located in seven pre-established points of our body. Hence the idea of separation, the illusory reality of the mind that creates the dualism between its different sensory perceptions.

Our mind, not being able to understand the reality of the Whole, simplifies this by separating it into distinct parts. Yet all that exists in time and space, both the beautiful and the ugly, the good and the bad, the high and the low, etc. is nothing but the univocal manifestation of the same reality.

For example, if we could 'see' the energy, there would be no darkness and light, because we would only see a vibration. If we want to start a real healing process within us, we must become aware of the All that inhabits us. We must understand that reality is not what we believe we see, because it is the projection of our inner world (veil of Maya). Only by overcoming the limits of judgment can we rediscover that we are ONE with each manifestation of the creative energy and that by accepting and loving our shadow areas, we can truly aspire to truly know each other and to complete ourselves in our very essence.

"If we take what we deny, we won't throw it out." **Gopi Krishna**

Unity is within us, it is what heals us, what sustains us in balance between apparently ambivalent forces. In our mind, shadow can become light through the harmonisation of the different polarities of thought. Unity is our own breath and it is Love that welcomes and completes everything.

CHAPTER 19

THE VIVO METHOD

Over the years, I have created several exercises for the easy learning of Reiki, as I strongly believe that this ancient Japanese art may be able to open secret doors of consciousness that are yet to be explored. In addition to the Akashic meditation below, I have also provided a learning methodology based on two easy evolutionary energy techniques.

I created this meditation with Hon Sha Ze Sho Nen, to send remote Reiki to situations from our past that have traumatized us in some way. By visiting the Akashic archives, these traumas can be resolved with the help of the third symbol.

AKASHIC DREAM MEDITATION

Let's start breathing in and out very slowly, rhythmically and constantly...

In and out...

In and out...

In and out...

Let us completely allow our thoughts to abandon our minds, let's breath in and out in and out...

Let's visualise our chakras slowly opening toward the sky, one by one...

we visualise the first chakra, the root chakra, an intense red colour permeating all around us...

Then the second chakra, the sacral chakra that slowly opens and releases a sparkling orange light...

We feel the expansion of the solar plexus chakra, the third chakra, and we take note of the strength of this chakra and its strong yellow energy. Moving up to our heart chakra, our fourth chakra, we expand universal love and love for ourselves in our heart space. We are aware of a beautiful green and pink energy that opens in our chest and pervades our being. Allow yourself to feel overcome by this divine energy of universal love.

We then go to the throat chakra, which is a strong blue energy; this energy opens us up to divine communication. Let this strong and creative energy clean and purify all the stagnated energy in our life.

Next, we we arrive at the sixth chakra, the third eye, whose colour is purple. This is the window of the soul that opens wide before us and it is here that we are see our guardian angels, our spirit guides, and other multidimensional beings around us.

Moving higher, we get to the crown chakra, the magnificent white lotus flower we have above our head. This is the antenna that allows us to receive and translate all the messages from the universe. We are here to listen to the messages that the universe wants to send us.

And now that all the chakras are open and rotating in the right direction, we visualize a huge Hon Sha Ze Sho Nen, the third Reiki Symbol, entering inside us through the chakra of the crown and – like a magnet – it collects all the energies we want to dissipate and release.

Hon Sha Ze Sho Nen has now become our guide on this journey. This symbol is the guide that will lead us on an extraordinary path; a path of discovering ourselves. We perceive it around us, we perceive it alongside us, we feel it everywhere. The symbol is our guide and our key to opening the treasure chest of our life. It is Hon Sha Ze Sho Nen who is leading us up through our body and out through the crown chakra.

We are out, and we look at the immense universe before us. We travel higher and higher. Our Symbol Guide takes us higher and higher… until we arrive at our destination. We have arrived at the Akashic Library, the library that contains many millions of books concerning all the souls that have lived in any dimension before us. Each of us has our own book and we have come to this place to consult our book.

Hon Sha Ze Sho Nen stays close to guide us through this amazing adventure; to be our trusted guide on this journey.

Finally, we see before us a huge wooden door. It opens up in front of us and we find we have arrived at this magnificent and unique circular library where all the records of all the souls are kept.

We are completely awestruck by the wonder of this incredible place. We are completely stunned by the many energies we find in this sacred place; where everything is beauty, joy and harmony.

We have come to a magical place.

There are angels and archangels. There are guides that accompany other souls to read their books. There are hundreds of Hon Sha Ze Sho Nen symbols that bring peace, comfort, light and harmony.

Keep breathing as we ask for our book to come to us… slowly, from a shelf, a book starts floating its way over to us. Notice what the book looks like. Is it heavy? Is it old and worn, or new and neat? Is it thin or thick? What colour is your book? What is it made of? Leather? Velvet? Is it a rolled-up scroll? We take notice, trying to understand and remember this.

Now, mentally, we ask the book to open to the pages of our current life.

We ask that the pages turn back to the past of this lifetime.

We ask the the remote Reiki symbol to take us back to the past and heal the many issues we remember; the unresolved trauma and painful experiences.

We ask the remote Reiki symbol to heal past situations; to heal relationships with people from the past; to help us forgive situations, things, people.

It is sometimes a painful journey but this process helps us move faster in our current situation. It's a journey we must undertake to heal these situations and to live a more serene and quieter life going forwards. So we ask Hon Sha Ze Sho Nen to help us along this path and accompany us back to these challenging times in our life so that our present and therefore our future may be different and more harmonious.

Slowly, as we bring ourselves back to the most recent pages of our current life, we find even heavier pages are opening up from the past. These are the pages of your most traumatic past lives and you are going to clear and release these past experiences right now with the help of Hon Sha Ze Sho Nen.

Breath slowly and deeply.

Breath in and out.

After a while, it is time to think about our current life; today's life. We then ask the book to open to a fresh, clean page and it is from here that our new life will begin. A new chapter in our life. The book is already filling with images that are part of our existence from this moment on. We have a look but we do not read everything.

Let us carry on from the energy that these images give us.

We observe all the projects we dream of; witness them all happening, beautifully unfolding, one by one with the help of Divine planning.

Always remember to include the Divine in our journeys and our book will be written as we go along in our life. Our story will be brighter and more luminous than ever

before. We are living the life we have always dreamt of. Keep breathing and visualize situations and challenges in your life already transforming in the most beautiful and positive way.

You feel lighter and lighter.

Breathe in and out.

Breathe in and out.

And now, we begin to slowly return. Our book is magically returned to the shelf and we start the journey back.

Hon Sha Ze Sho Nen lovingly guides us back to our life on the Earth today. We are happy and content and we are slowly coming back into our body.

One by one, each of our chakras spin and rotate in the correct direction.

We bring ourselves gently back to the room and make some small movements with our feet and legs, hands and arms.

We take a deep inhale and exhale, and slowly open our eyes, welcoming the new dawn of our new glorious life.

THE REIKI GRID OF WISHES

The Reiki Grid is a method I developed for remotely sending Reiki to specific situations or projects in the future. I developed it for my second level Reiki students to be used after they've received the level two attunements.

For beginners to this work, it's better to start with simple projects or situations you would like to address and solve. When you've got the hang of the process, you can move on to more complex projects.

The Reiki Grid is a way of learning symbols to create our reality. As already mentioned in the book bestselling book *The Secret* by Rhonda Byrne, we are able to ask the Universe and get whatever we desire: it is sufficient, however, that our wishes are for the maximum benefit of the person making the request.

The technique involves drawing three Reiki symbols on a sheet of rectangular paper.

To start, take a rectangular sheet of paper on which you draw the Hon Sha Ze Sho Nen symbol in the centre. Then you draw the Sei He Ki symbol, for releasing emotional blockage, at the four corners. Finally, you draw the Cho Ku Rei light vortex symbol in the middle of each side.

Write down the project you want to fulfil inside the grid and send remote Reiki to the project in the future for three consecutive days, at the same time and with the same vibration.

Repeat the exercise every week for three days in a row, until the project has been fulfilled.

It is important that – once Reiki has been sent – you no longer think about the project. You should leave it in the ether, in touch with the Infinite, and leave it in the hands of the Universe to bring into reality.

When the project is completed, the sheet will be burned, returning it through the wind to the Universe.

The grid of wishes can be used only if you have been activated by someone who has themselves been attuned to its activation.

Educating people about Reiki is, in my opinion, a rather difficult task and not because Reiki is a difficult technique to learn, but because the word 'Reiki' has been abused and misused in the past years, so my work in seeding and changing people's opinion on Reiki is difficult, but not impossible.

I have lived for several years in Great Britain and the United States where Reiki is widely used as a healing technique, in some countries though it is still exchanged for something that goes against any form of religions and people stay away from it, without considering that Reiki is only Love, and it is only a channeling healing experience and nothing else.

THE SEI HE KI BOX
I have created this exercise, which I have called the Sei He Ki box, because many people ask me how to protect themselves from energy-sapping people and situations.

Every morning, before you leave home, and once you have centred yourselves with Reiki energy, envisage yourself in white light and imagine yourself being enclosed in a Sei He Ki cube.

Visualise the Sei He Ki symbol in front of you, behind you, beside you, above your head and underneath your feet.

Imagine yourselves inside the box, so that nothing and no-one can come close to you to suck your energy or enter your aura. Remember that this is the best time to have your aura completely expanded and free from marks left by other people. It is, therefore, very important that you always protect yourselves with Sei He Ki.

SWEEPING THE AURA

Before starting treatments, it is a good idea to sweep the aura of the person you are about to treat.

The aura is a set of bioenergetic waves that flow around our body and extend a few centimetres beyond the boundaries of the physical body.

The aura can be divided into layers. There is the etheric layer, the emotional, mental, astral, celestial and causal layers.

Whenever we come into contact with things, animals and people, our auras exchange information held in these layers.

When we sweep the aura, by running our hands just above the body from head to toe, we touch the etheric layer of the aura, which is the first energy body and which extends just beyond the physical body in coloured, electromagnetic waves.

During the Reiki treatment, then, by 'sweeping' the aura, we come into contact with its vibrations and frequencies.

At the beginning of the treatment, the person's body is swept from head to toe, about 10 centimeters from the physical body to connect with both the physical body and the subtle layers of the energy body.

The therapist thus gently connects with the energy of the person to be treated and also helps them relax.

SELF-REIKI TREATMENT

The first treatment that you learn in Reiki is how to give a treatment to youself.

It is beneficial to practice Reiki on yourself to familiarise with the new energy.

You can start in the morning. The treatment will be energizing and will provide a sense of well-being throughout the day. You can also practice a self Reiki treatment in bed, before falling asleep in the evening. By working only with the higher chakras you will feel a sense of tranquility, especially if the day has been particularly stressful. It may be that when you wake up, you find your hands are still in the Reiki positions. Stay for five minutes on each position. Remember to move your hands one at a time as you move from one position to another. Treat all parts of the body that need healing energy. To finish, get into a sitting position and place your hands over your heart centre to connect with the universal energy.

Place your hands on your heart chakra to centre yourself. (Fig.0)
Place your hands on both cheeks for at least three minutes. (Fig.1)
Place your hands on your ears. (Fig.2)
Place your hands over your eyes. (Fig.3)
Place one hand on the forehead and the other on the back of the neck. (Fig.4)
Place your hands on top of your head (Fig. 5)
Place the hand that was on the forehead on the throat and leave the other on the back of the neck. (Fig.6)
Place your hands on your chest. (Fig.7)
Place your hands on the solar plexus, just above the navel. (Fig.8)
Place your hands on the sacral chakra, just below the navel. (Fig.9)
Place your hands over the genitals (root chakra). (Fig.10)
Place your hands on your thighs. (Fig.11)
Place your hands on your knees. (Fig. 12)
Place the right leg on the left leg, keeping one hand on the right knee and the other on the right ankle. (Fig. 13)

Place your hands on the back and front of your right foot. (Fig.14)
Place the left leg on the right leg keeping one hand on the left knee and the other on the left ankle. (Fig. 15)
Place your hands on the back and front of your left foot. (Fig 16)
Place your hands on your kidneys. (Fig 17)
Return to the heart centre position. (Fig. 18)

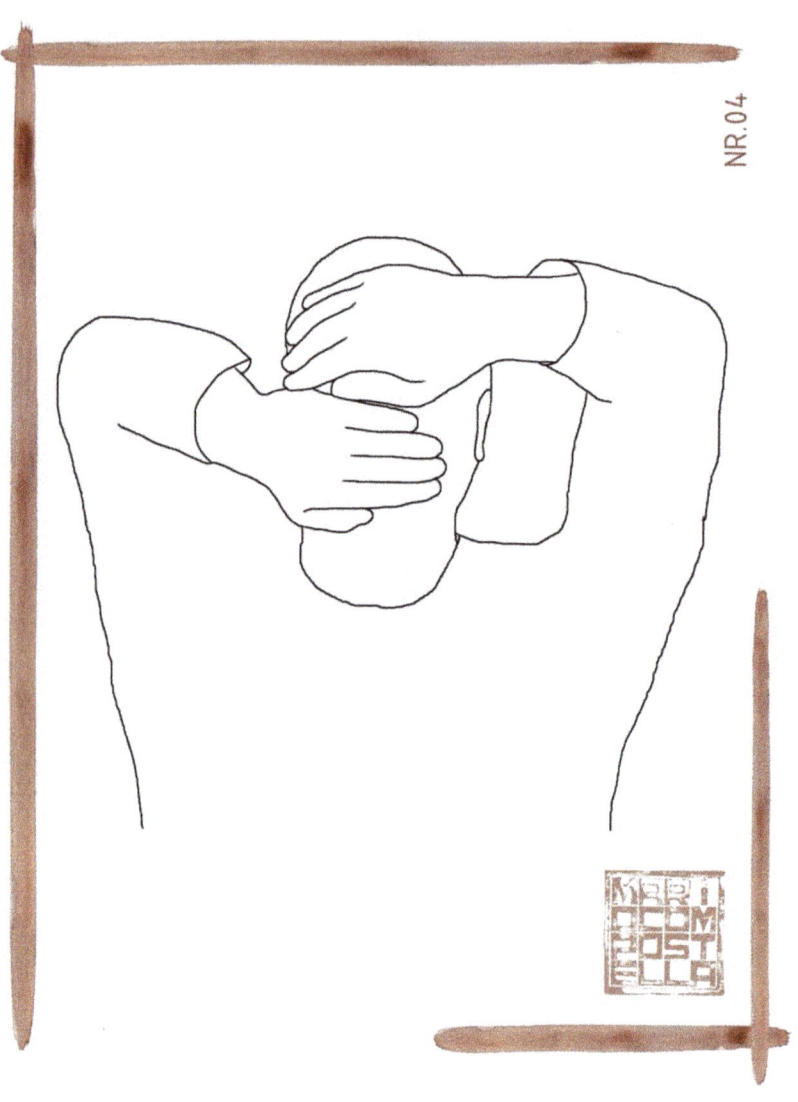

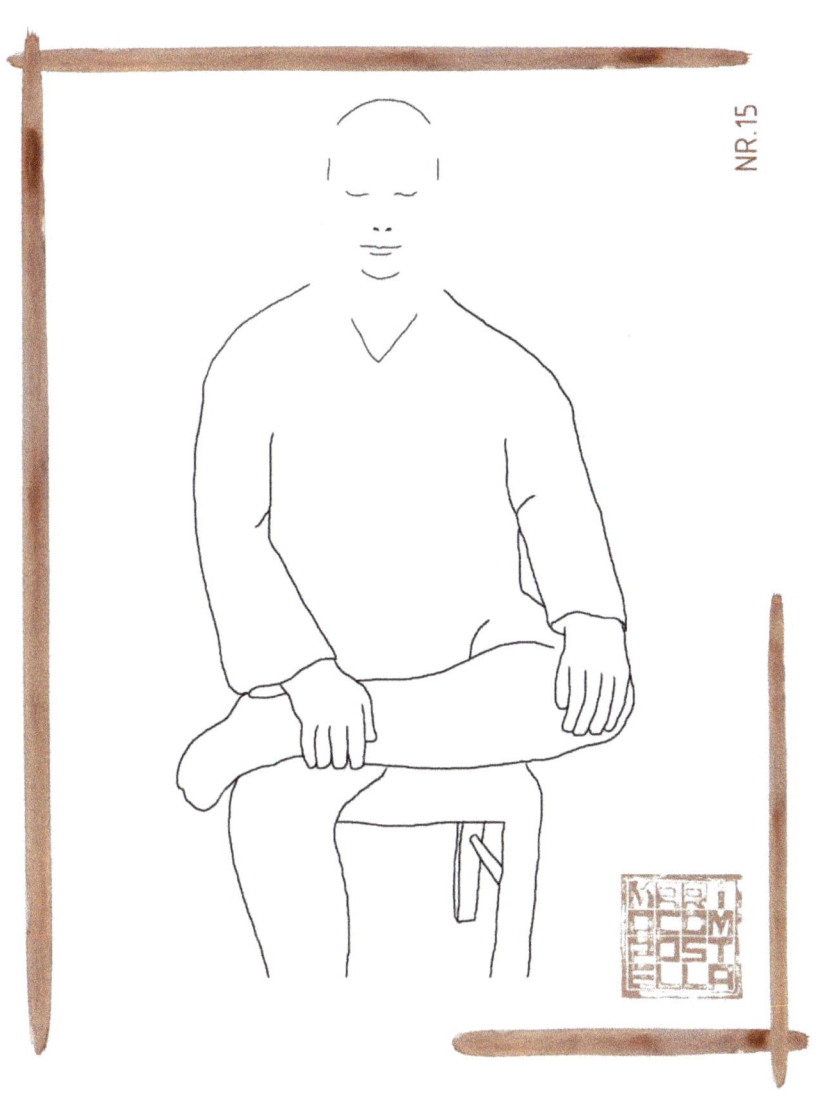

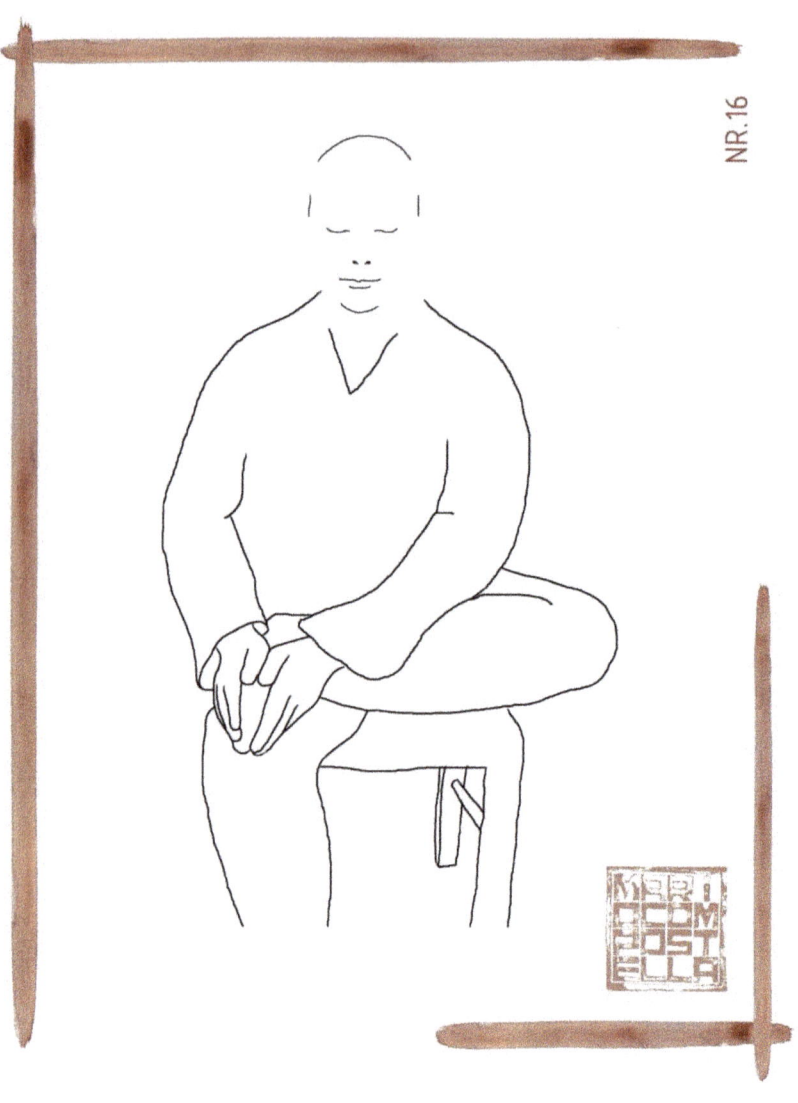

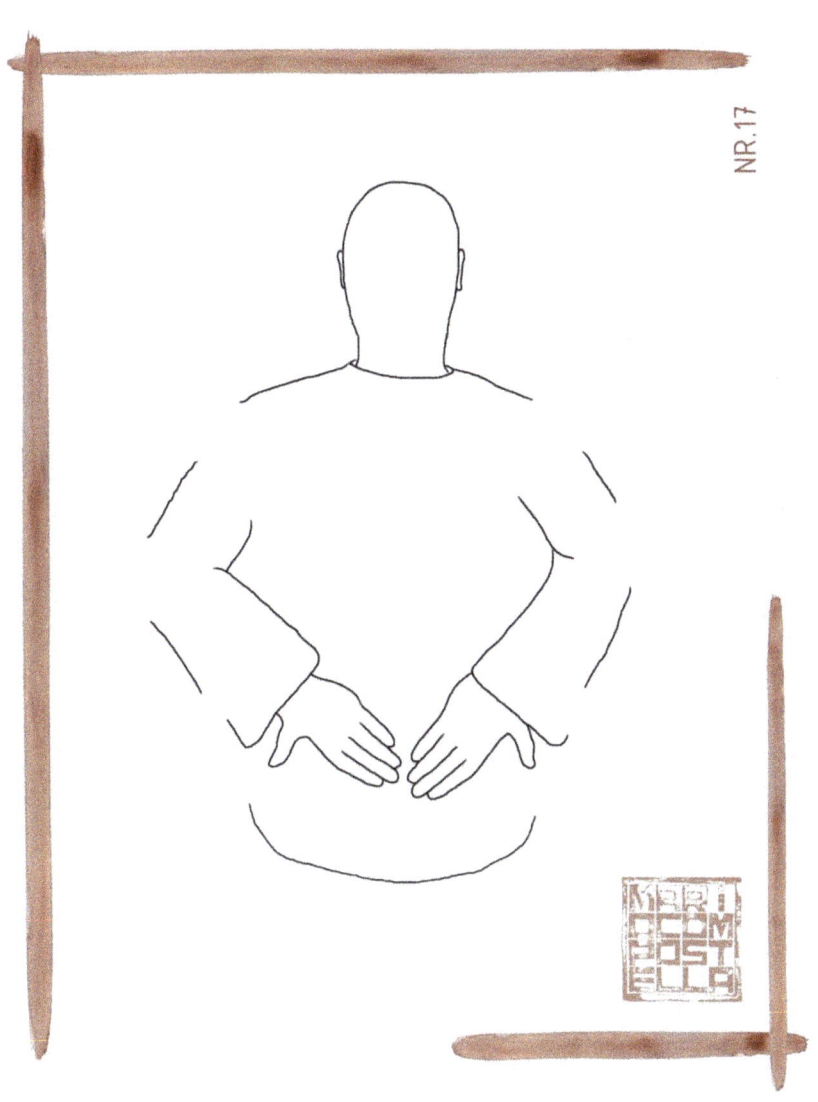

CHAPTER 20

GIVING REIKI

Reiki is available to all those people who wish to receive it. It's a tool for people who wish to grow spiritually and are willing to take responsibility for their own life.

Reiki helps both those who receive it and those who practice it by creating a state of peace and harmony, well-being and energetic balance.

Reiki stimulates both physical and psychic healing processes.

Whenever a Reiki treatment is practiced it is a good practice to wash your hands before and after the session.

Water is an excellent element of purification and eliminates all unwanted energies.

The client is invited to lie down, comfortably dressed, on a therapy bed after taking off metal objects on their person, such as jewelry, belts, coins, etc. This way the energy will flow more freely.

Treatment requires the patient and the therapist to be barefoot.

Soft music could make the session more relaxing.

PRELIMINARIES

First, the therapist places their hands over their own heart centre, to call upon the Universal Energy with the intention of healing the patient.

Imagine that your heart chakra is a big, green button. You push the button when you want the universal energy to start flowing. Press the button again when you want the energy to stop.

Begin by sweeping the aura of the patient, placing your hands a few inches above the recipient's body.

Begin at the crown chakra and move downward in a very slow and gentle motion.

I insist that this movement be slow to avoid causing damage or trauma to the person being treated. The first swipe is done in the centre of the body, a second and a third on the right and left of the body.

When caressing and stroking the aura, you can use one hand or both hands. While doing so, you may experience a series of sensations, such as coldness, heat, tingling in the hands, etc. that will indicate the client's energy blocks and the areas that need more energy.

This will be the first encounter with your patient's energy.

Always follow your intuition.

The aura is the energy field that surrounds every living being and when you caress the aura you feel the energy arriving.

Let your hands move freely without any restrictions or resistance. Don't focus too much. Feel free to receive the energy and pass it on to your patient.

Open your client's chakras in a circular motion a few centimeters above the body, rotating your hands in the direction in which the chakra turns. For females, first chakra is anti-clockwise.

At the end of the treatment, close the chakras with the same rotational movement, but in the opposite position to the direction of the chakras themselves.

It is necessary to receive attunements in order to have a connection with universal energy and be able to treat a person with Reiki. Attunement can only be received from a Reiki Master.

Keep yourself relaxed and always maintain physical contact with your patient. When you move from one position to another, always do it with one hand at a time, otherwise you will stop the flow of energy.

Reiki must be done without hand pressure so it is a very light and gentle touch. At the end of the treatment, mentally repeat three times in a row the words, 'Reiki off, Reiki off, Reiki off'.

HAND POSITIONS GIVING REIKI

Begin by placing your hands on your own heart chakra to centre yourself. (Fig 0)

Sit behind the person lying on the treatment table.

Move your hands one at a time and place them on their ears. The ears govern the bladder and some parts of the brain (Fig 2)

Place your hands over their eyes, crossing your thumbs, leaving the nose free, so that the patient can breathe easily. The eyes also represent the inner vision. (Fig 3)

Place your hands on their head (crown chakra).
By treating the head, the neurological and sensory systems are treated, furthermore the part of the body that first sees the light

during childbirth is treated and therefore, by unblocking it, the client's trust in the outside world is renewed. (Fig 4)

Place one hand on the side of their head and slowly turn the head to that side, supporting it with your hand. Put your other hand on the other side of the face and slowly turn the head back to centre, so both your hands can slide under to support the head from beneath. (Fig 5)

Place one hand on the back of their neck and move the other hand to their forehead. (Fig 6)

Leave one hand on the back of their neck and move the other on to the heart chakra. (Fig 7)

BODY
Put your hands on their shoulders. (Fig 8)

Place your V-shaped hands on the heart chakra. (Fig 9)

Stand up, leaving one hand on the person's body, moving to their side and placing both hands on the chest, just below the throat. (Fig 10)

The fingertips of one hand should touch the inside of the wrist of your other hand. This is the region of the heart, which gives rhythm to our body, and of the lungs, which give it breath.

Place your hands on their upper abdomen (solar plexus). (Fig 11)

Place your hands on their lower abdomen (sacral chakra). (Fig 12)

LEGS
Place your hands on their thighs. (Fig 13)
This is important for circulation and for the treatment of edema.

Place your hands on their knees. This helps the joints and mobility. (Fig 14)

Place your hands on their shins. (Fig 15)

Place your hands on their ankles. This corresponds to the neck and the back, which is why treating them affects the cervical area. (Fig 16)

Place your hands on the recipient's feet. The feet support the body and are the final part. (Fig 17)

Press with both thumbs on the centre of the soles of the feet to finish the front treatment. (Fig 18)
The chakras of the feet are the ones through which the 'junk' energy that has accumulated in the body comes out and that is why we always conclude the treatment on the feet.

Shake your hands three times to shake off the accumulated, unwanted energy.

Return to the patient's chest and place your hands a few inches above the chest to send the Reiki energy. (Fig.19)
This movement is for women only; for men, the chest can be accessed after working on the throat.

First chakra (genitals): On women, place your hands in a V shape a few centimeters above the body. For men, it is necessary to place your hands above the genitals, always far from the body. (Fig.20)
We DO NOT touch the genitals, we work on them from a distance.

Ask the receiver to turn over before working on the body from behind.

HEAD
Sit behind the person who is lying on the bed and place your hands on their head. (Fig. 21)

BODY
Put your hands on their shoulders. (Fig. 22)

Then you get up, always keeping one hand on the body and placing both hands in the middle of the dorsal area so that the fingertips of one hand can touch the wrist of the other (heart chakra). (Fig. 23)

Place your hands on their back to form a T-shape between the shoulder blades (one hand crosses the shoulders and the other is placed along the spine so that the fingers touch the hand). (Fig. 24) This position balances the upper chakras.

Rotate the right hand, towards the kidneys, and place both hands so that the fingertips of one hand can touch the wrist of the other. This part of the body acts on the adrenal glands, stomach, digestion and kidney function. (Fig. 25)

Form a second T-shape at the base of the back with one hand crossing the base of the spine and the other resting on the buttocks. This balances the lower Chakras. (Fig. 26)

LEGS (BACK)
Place your hands on the hamstrings at the back of the thighs. (Fig. 27)

Place your hands on the back of both knees with extreme delicacy as this is a very sensitive part of the body. We are working on the liver, pancreas, and kidneys. (Fig. 28)

Place your hands on the calves. (Fig. 29)

Place your hands on the ankles. (Fig. 30)

Place your palms on the soles of the recipient's feet in order to support them, thus working on all organs. (Fig. 31)

Return to the recipient's head and close the chakras starting with the first one, the root chakra. Make a rotating movement with your hands in the opposite direction to that in which the chakra rotates. (If your patient is a woman, you will close the root chakra by rotating your hand three times clockwise; if your patient is a man, you will do the opposite and so on).

Sweep the aura once in the middle of the person's body. Shake your hands three times, a few centimeters above the body, mentally saying: 'Reiki off, Reiki off, Reiki off'.

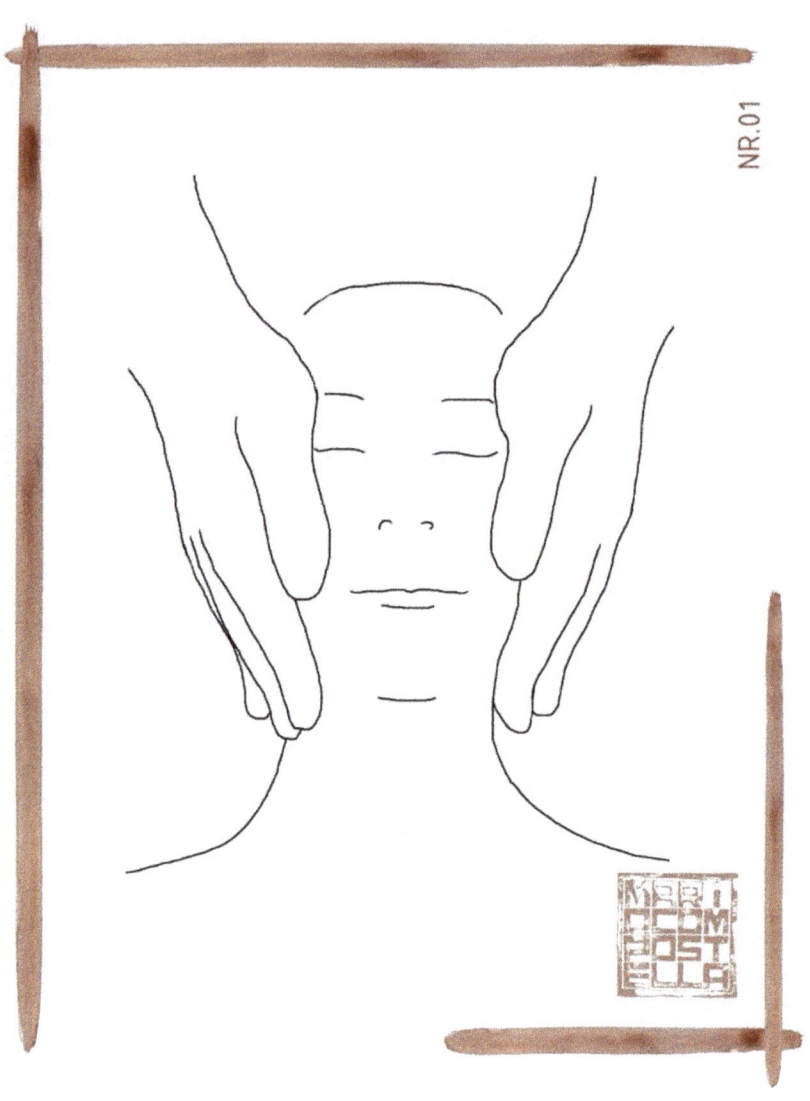

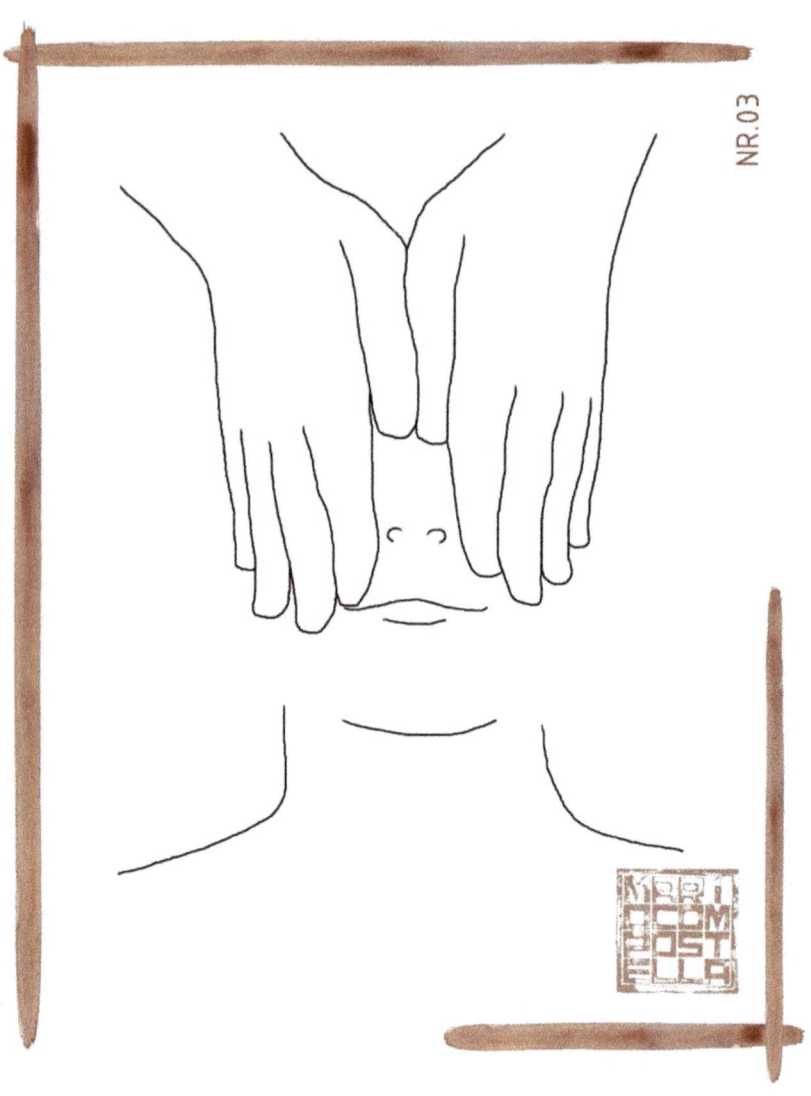

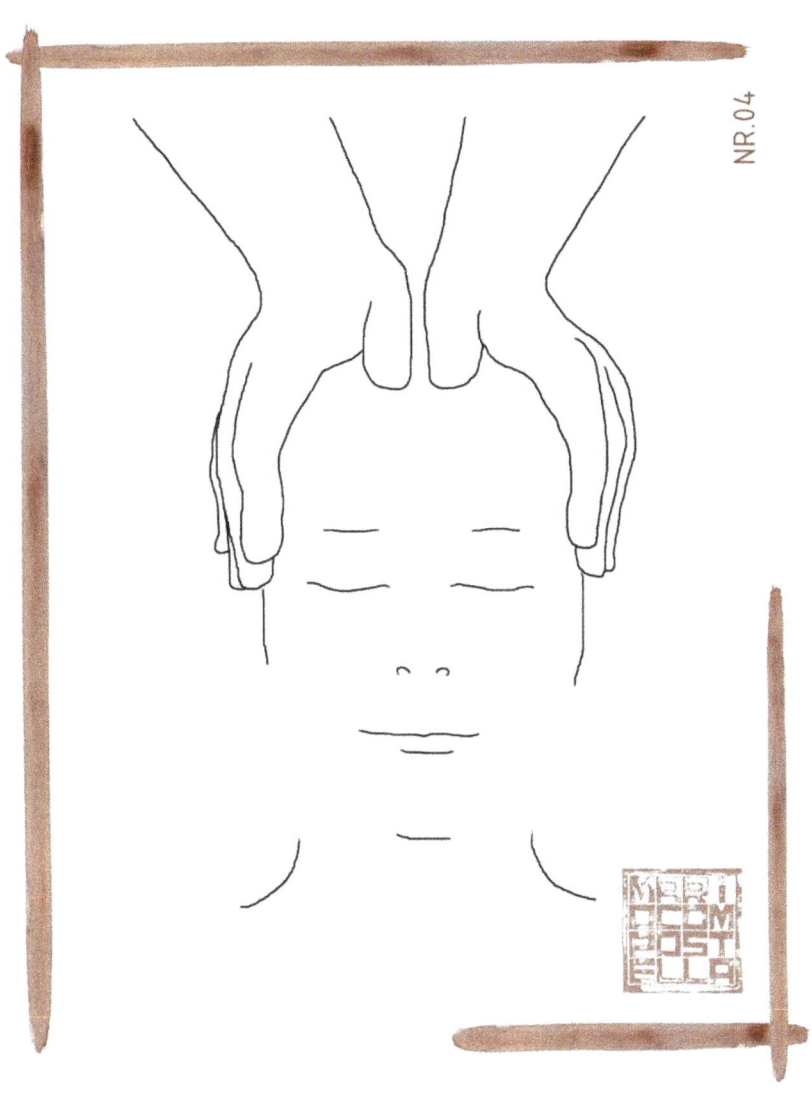

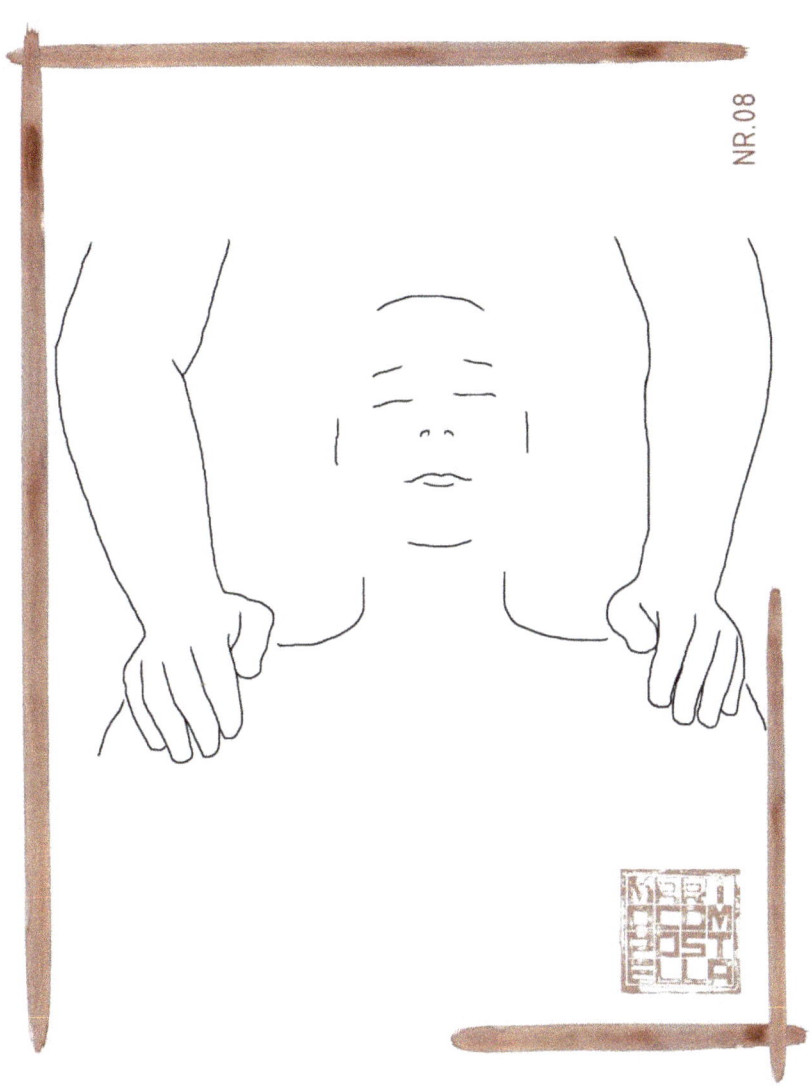

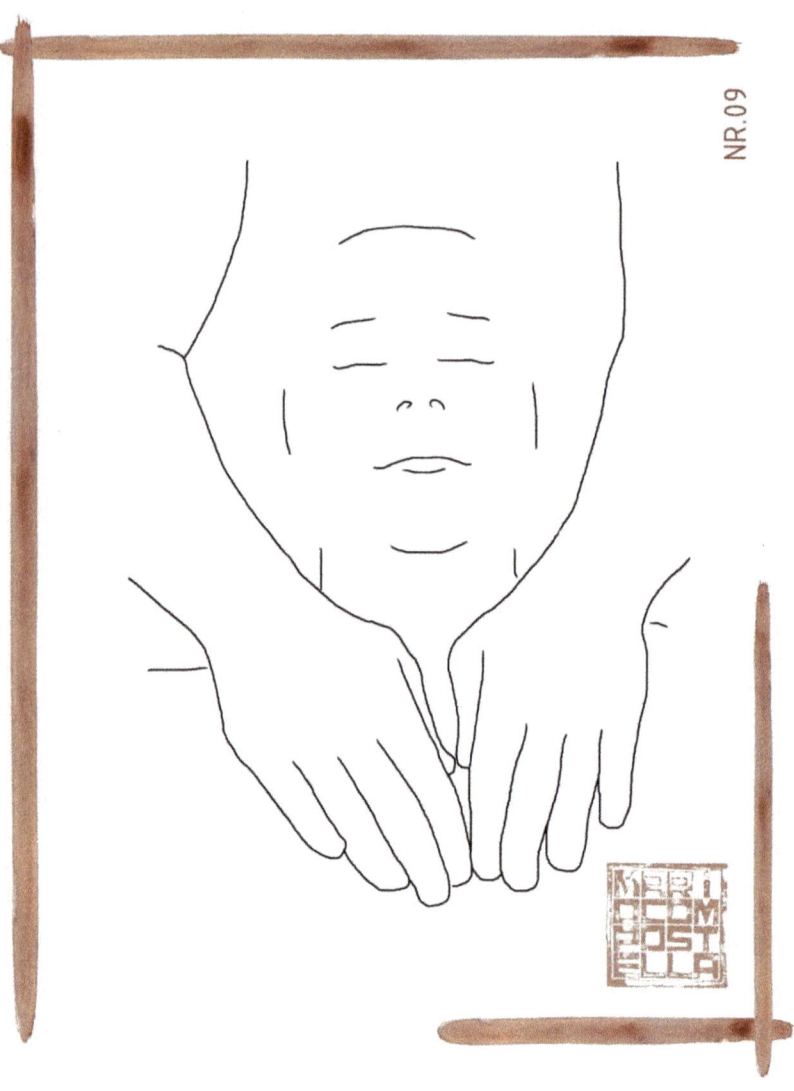

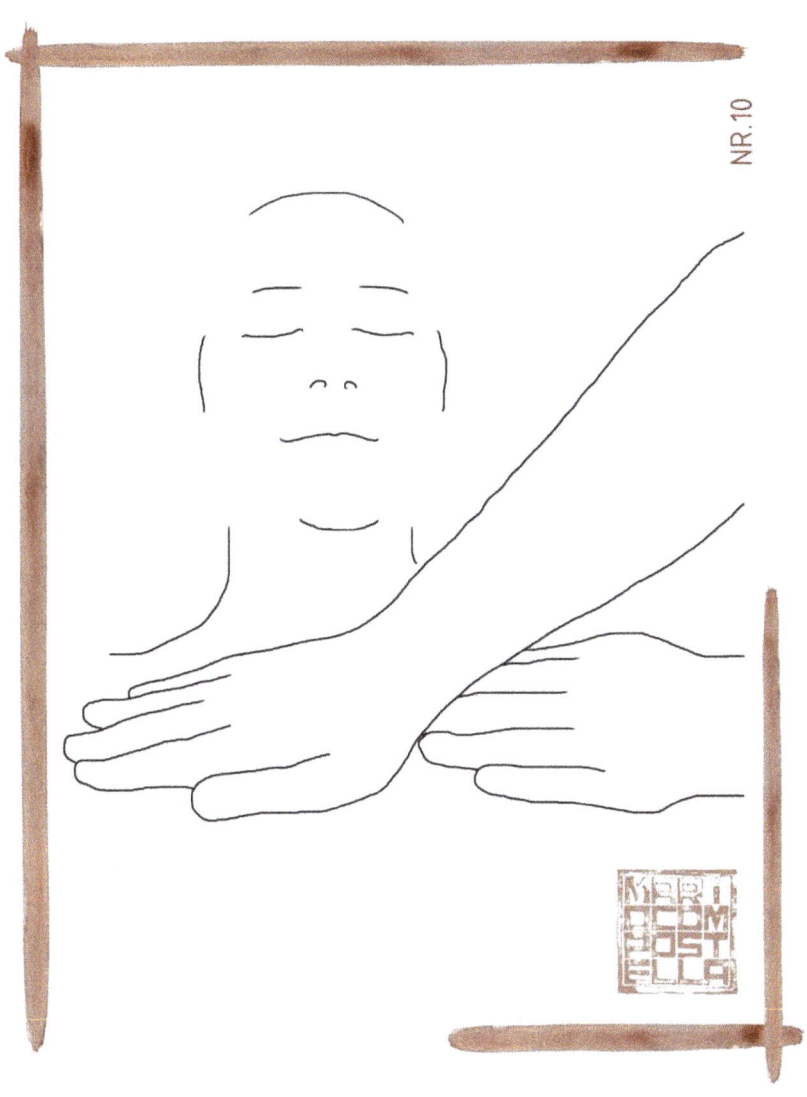

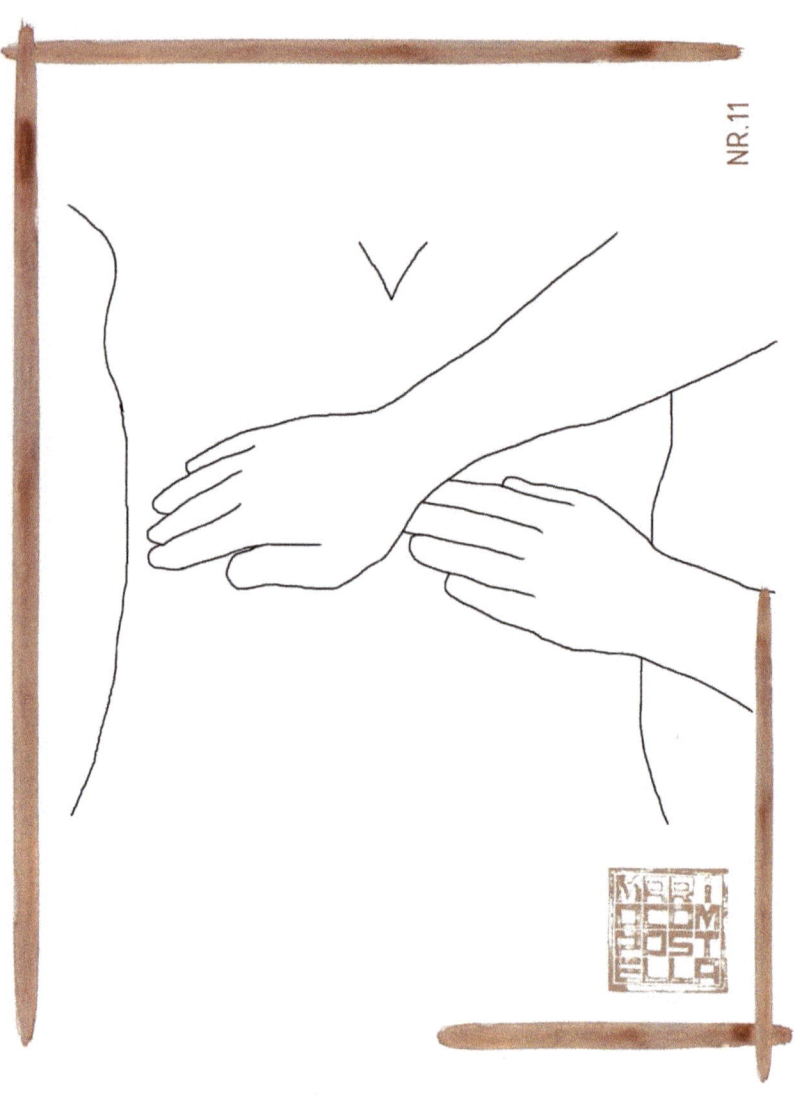

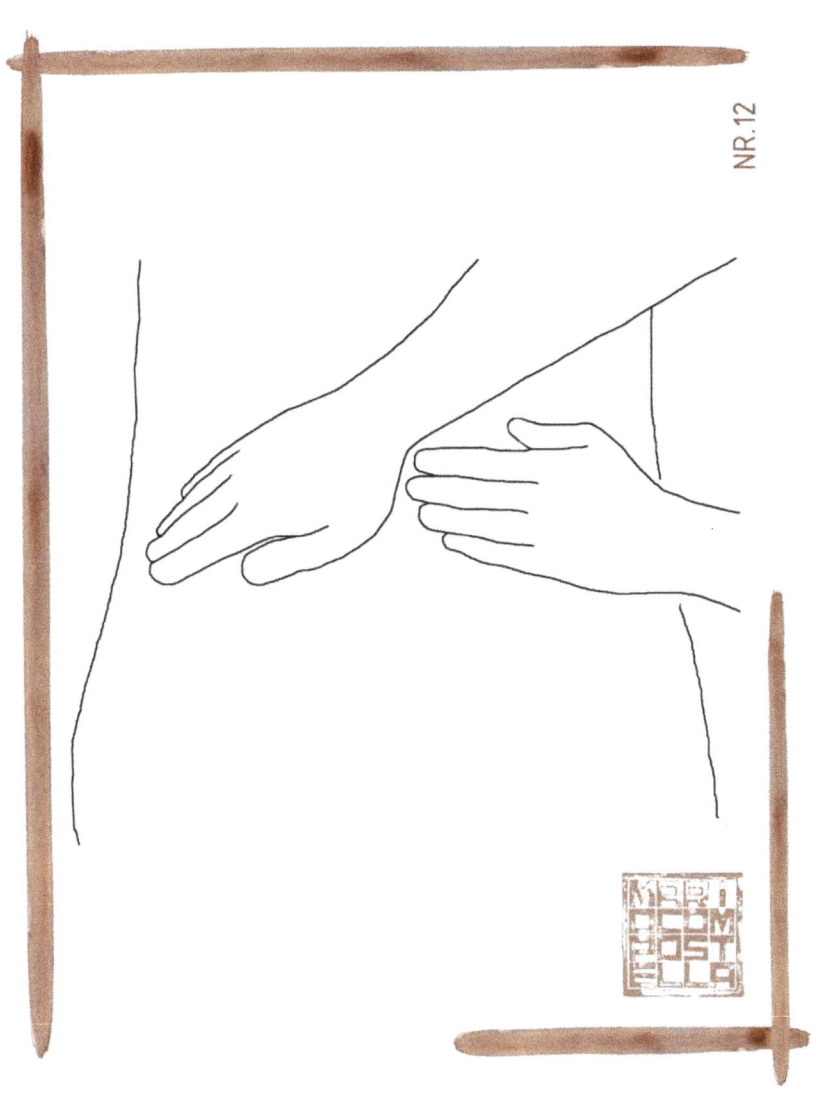

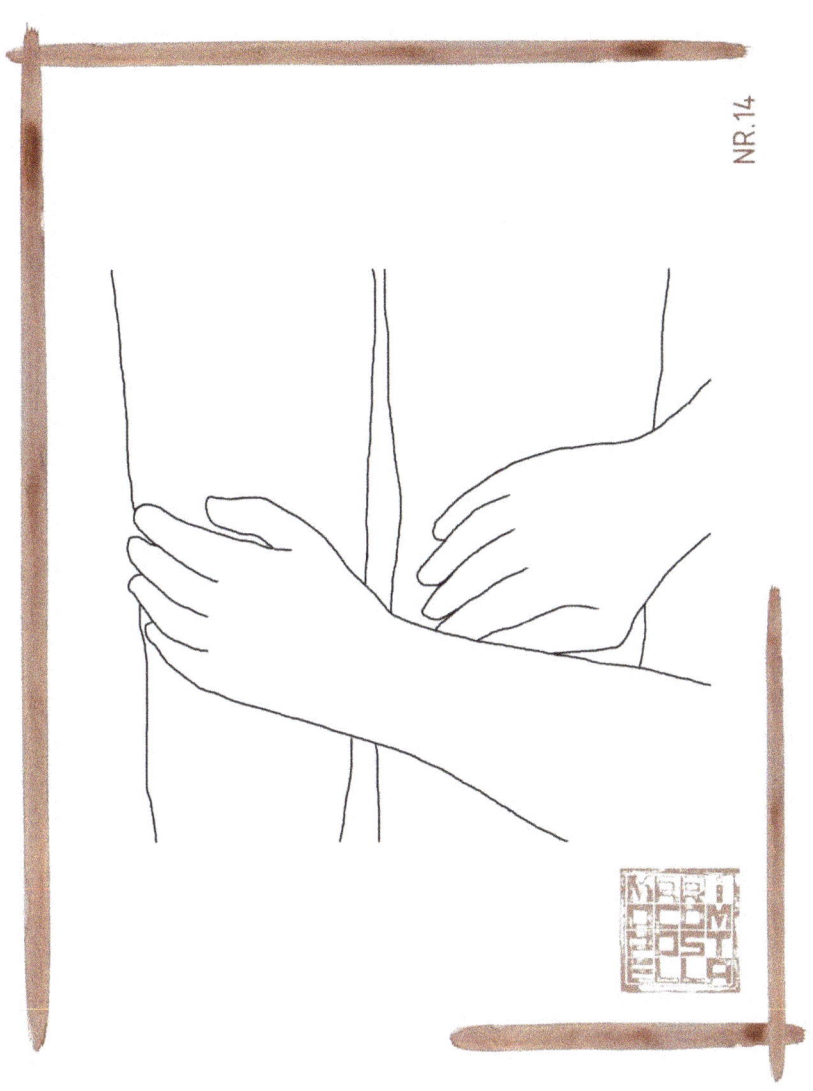

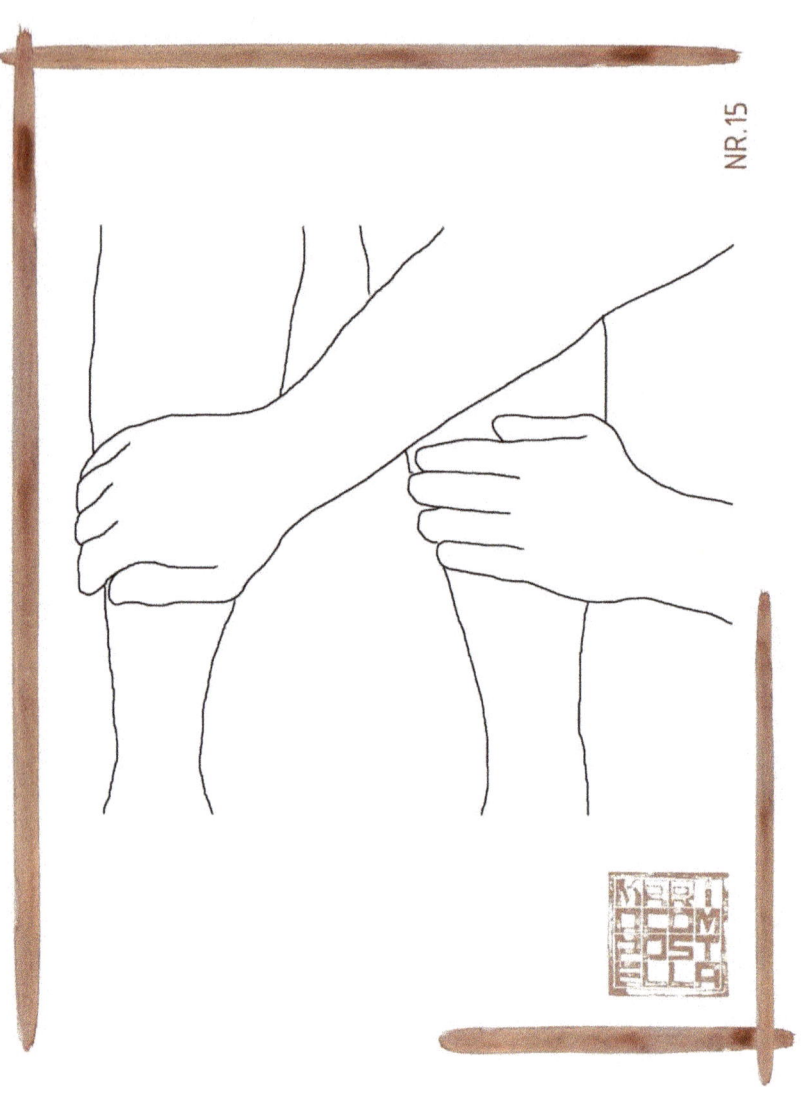

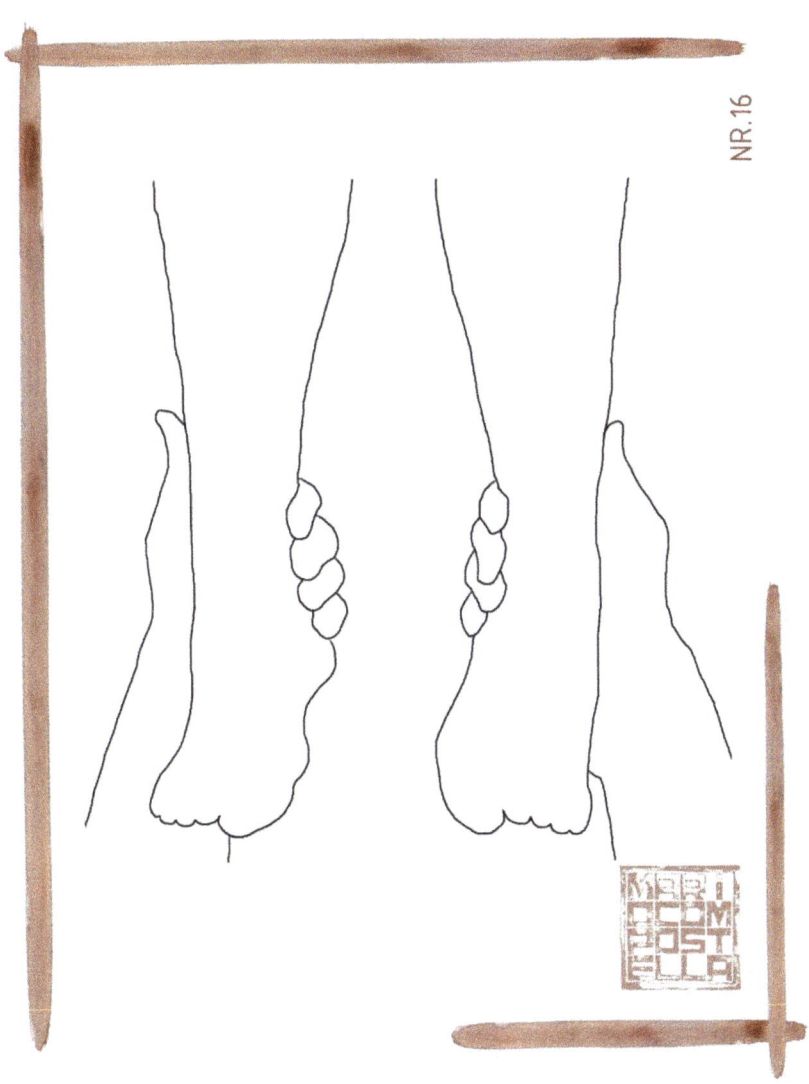

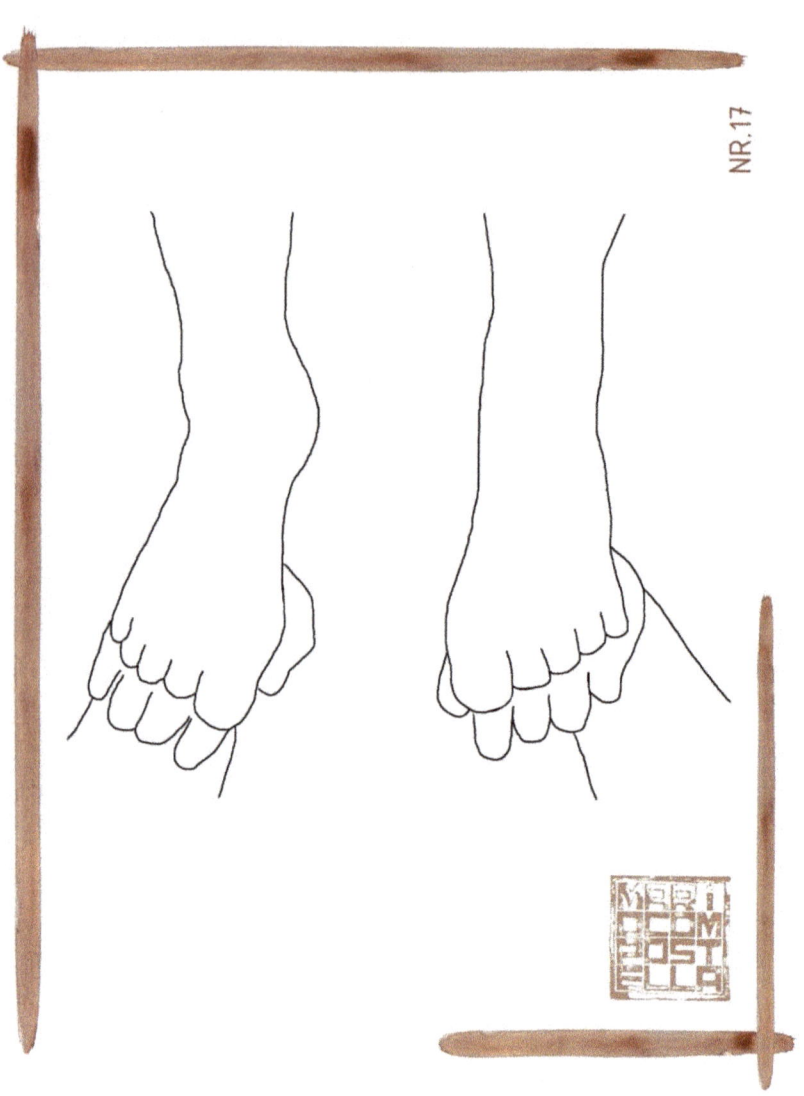

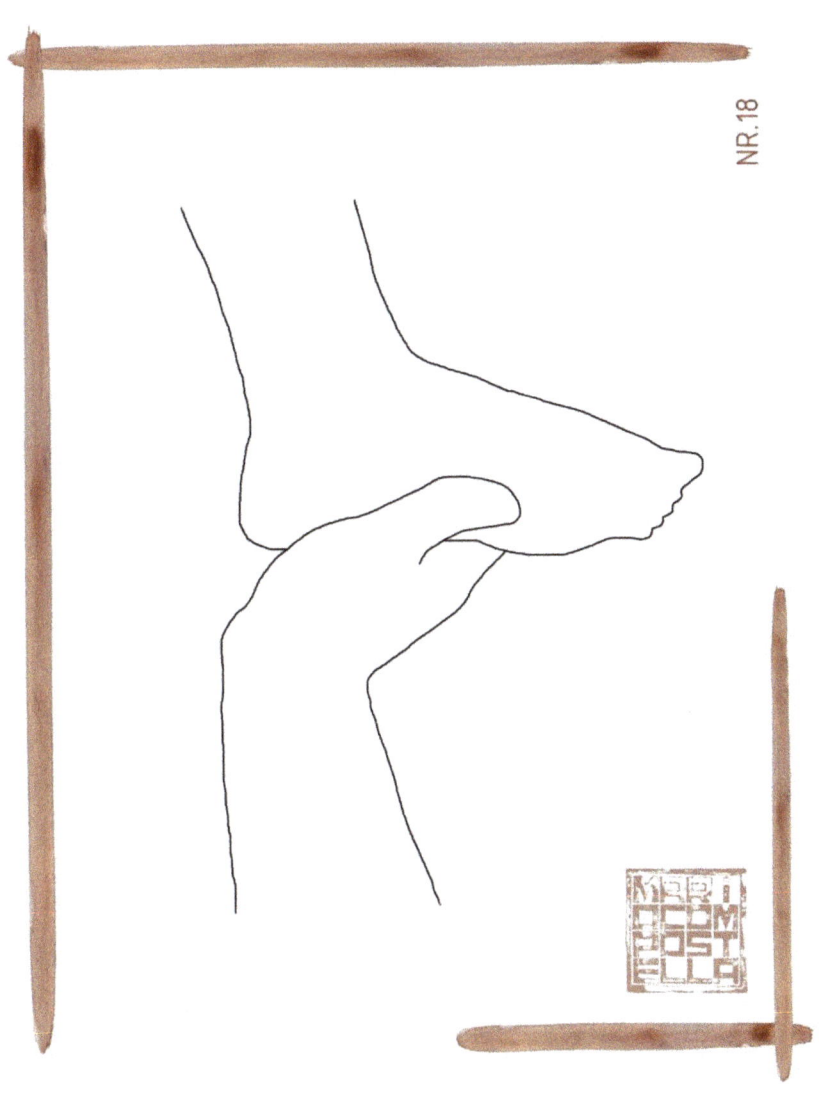

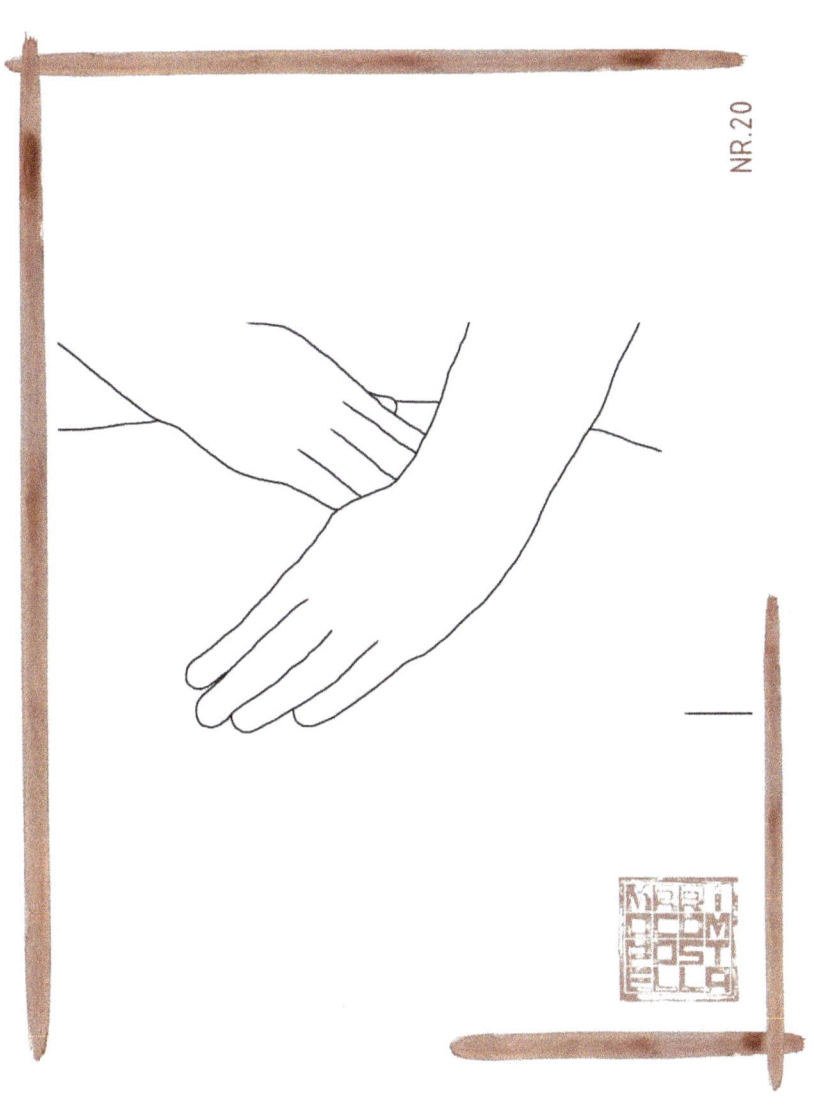

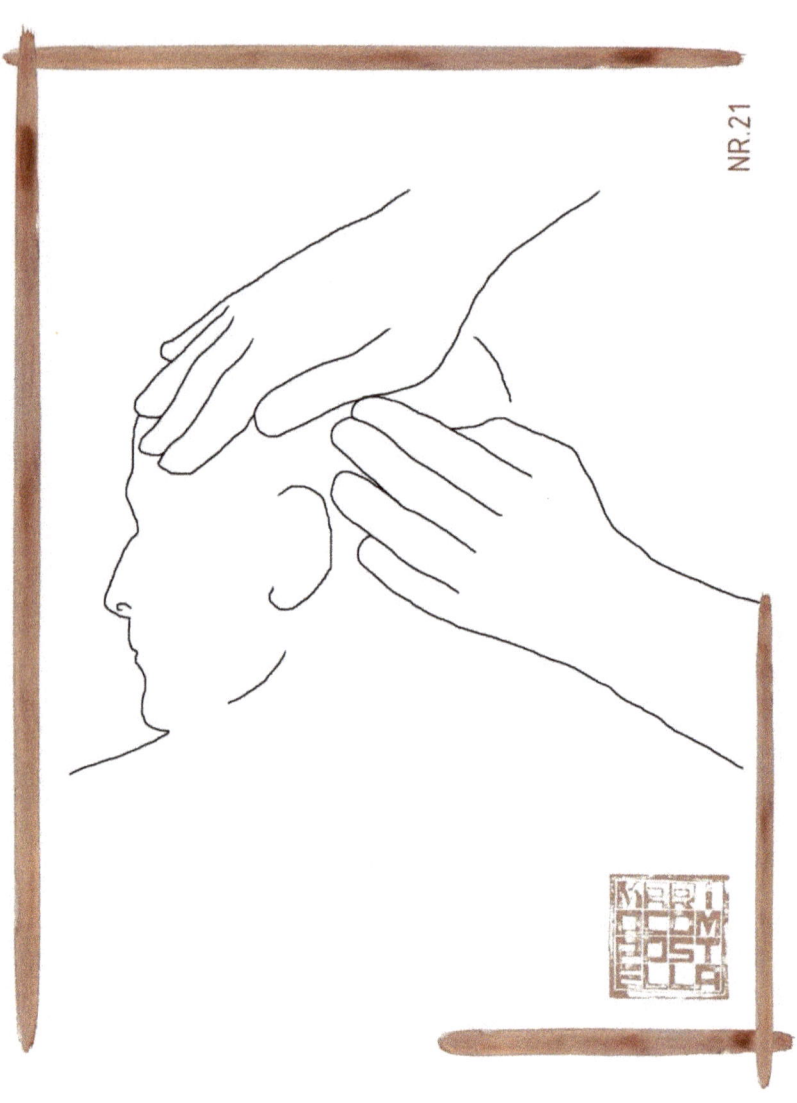

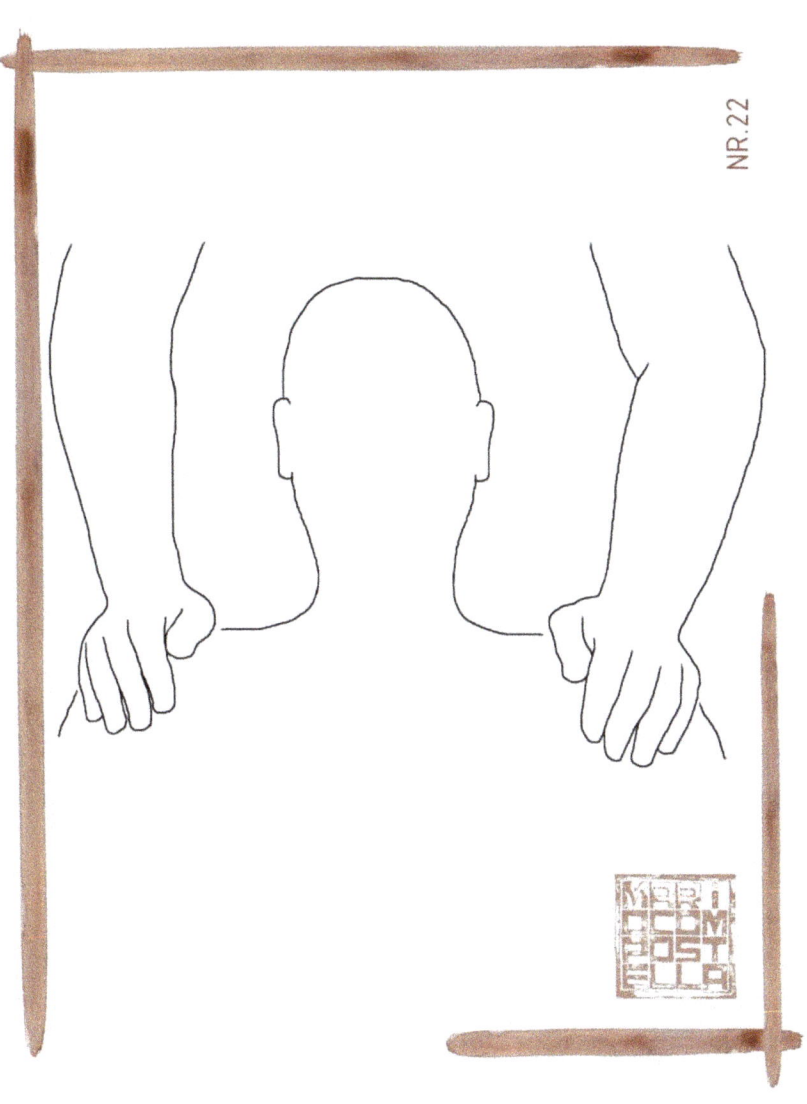

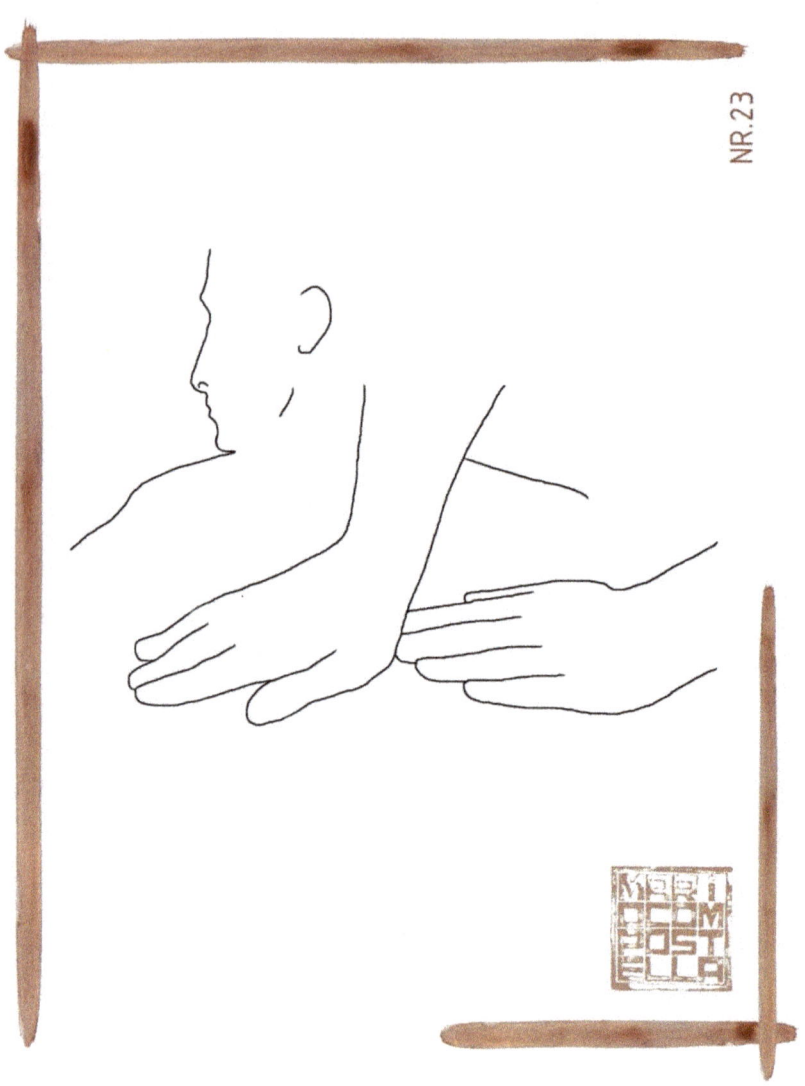

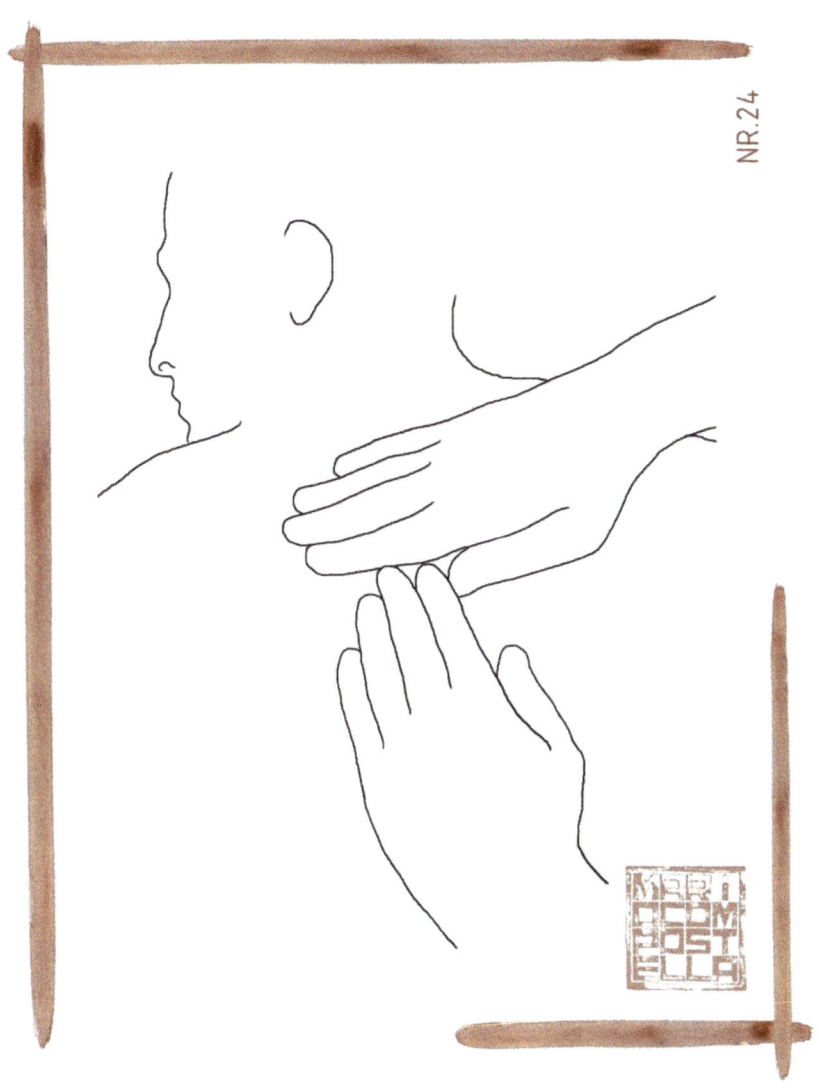

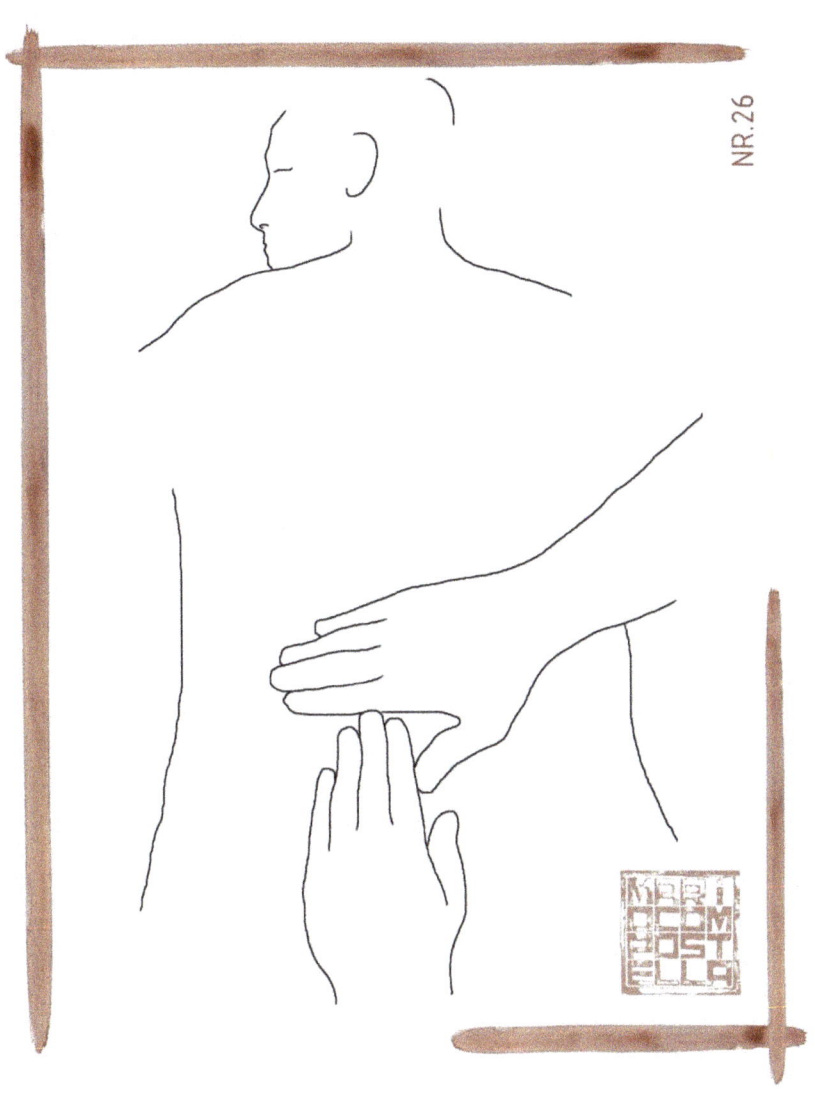

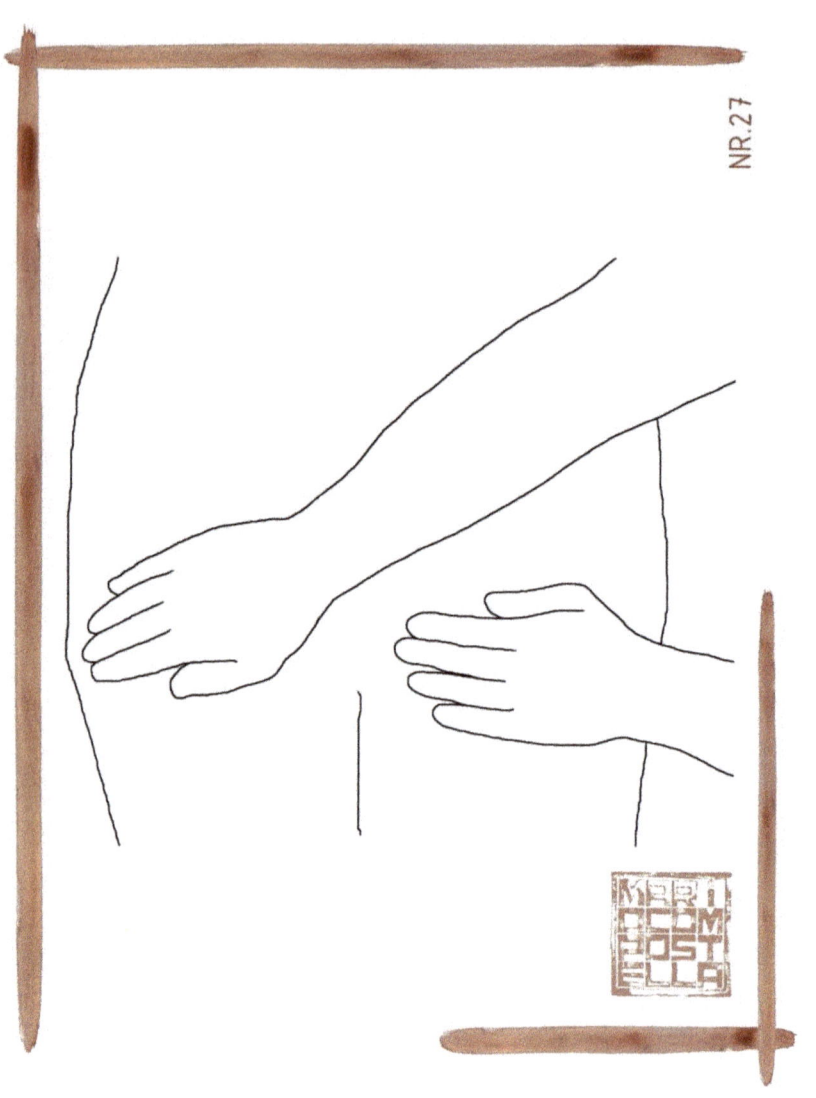

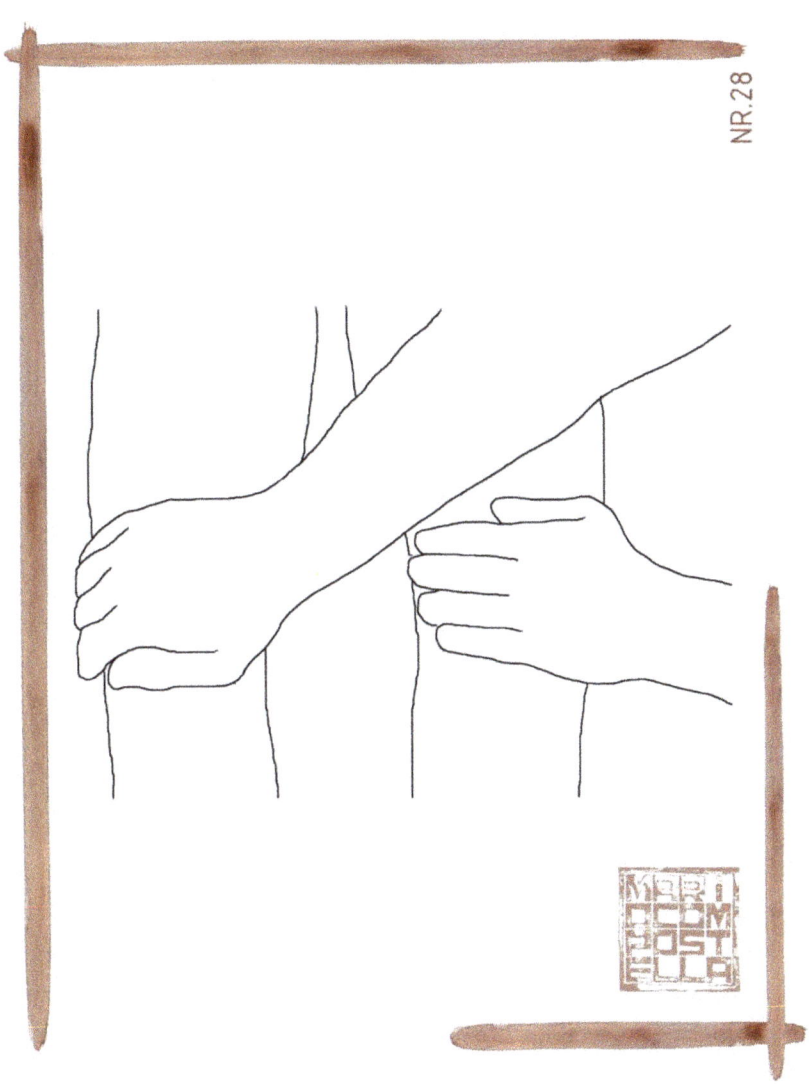

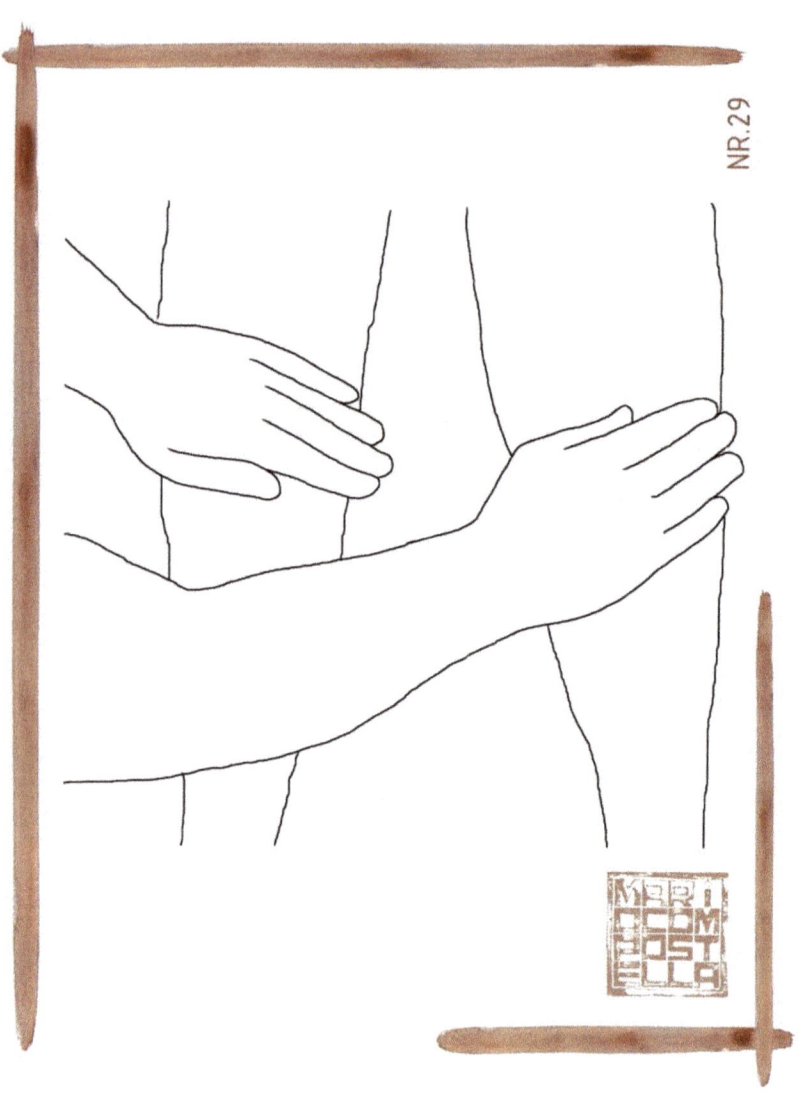

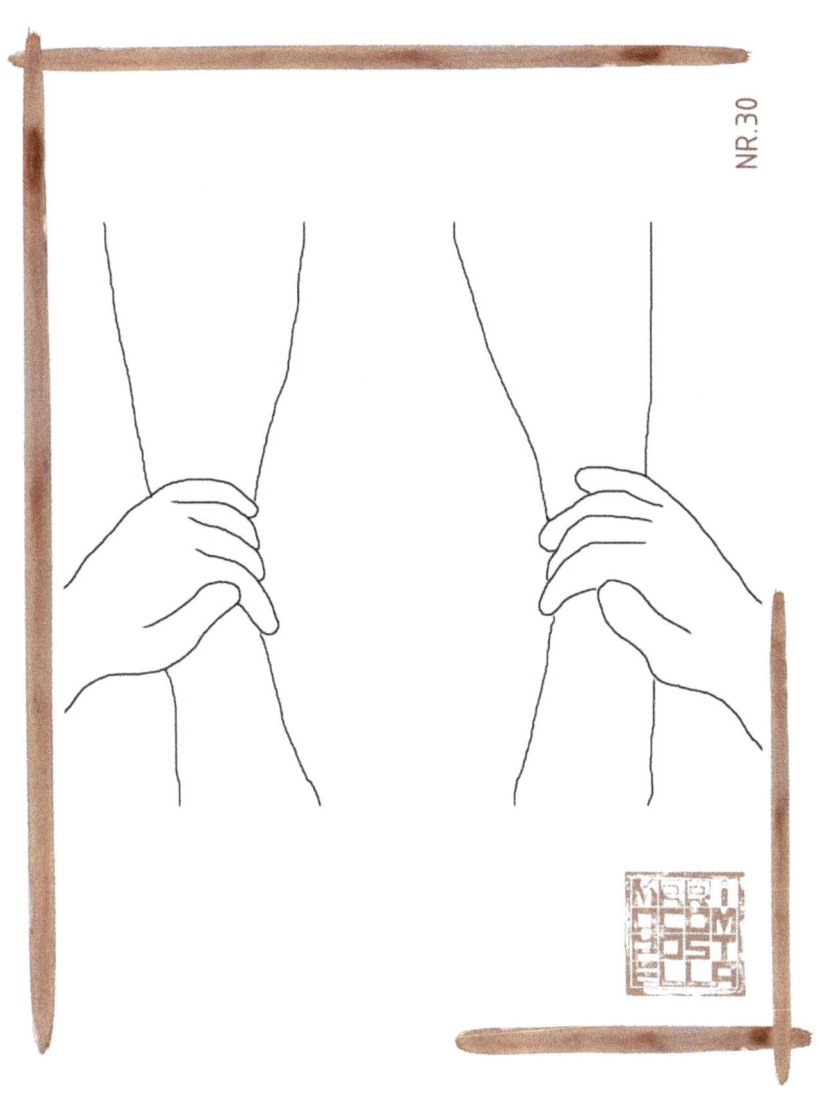

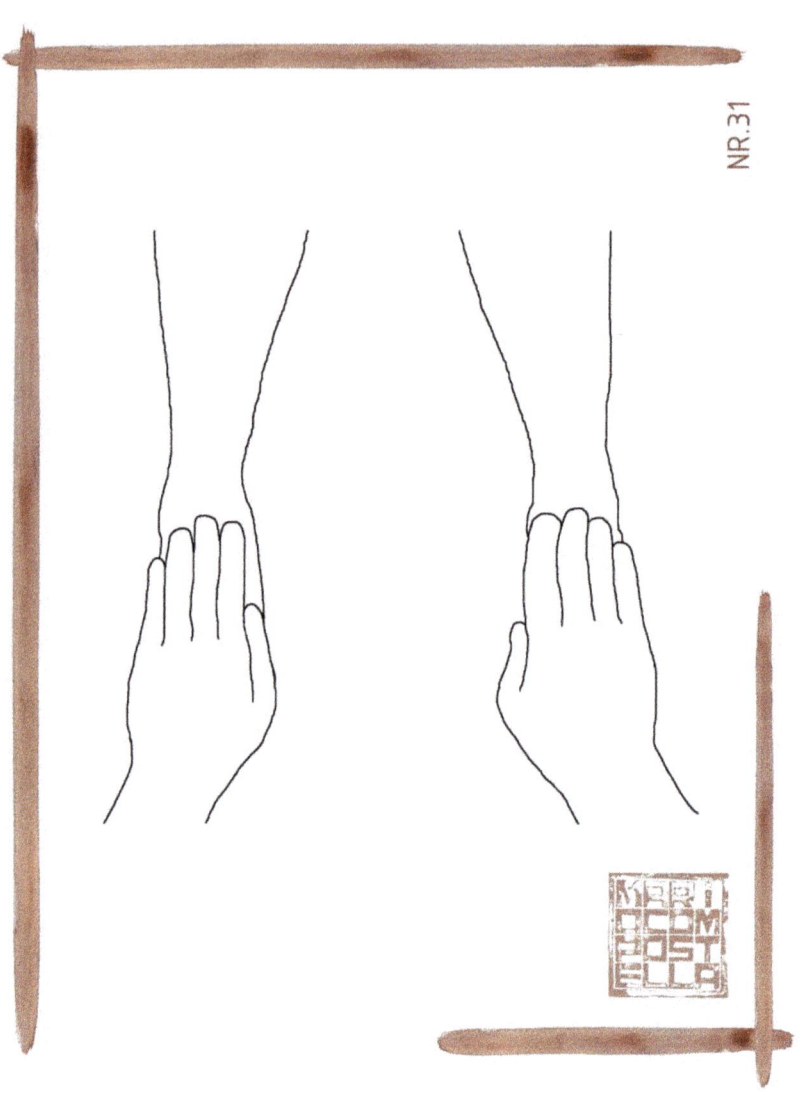

QUICK REIKI TREATMENT

If there is not much time available and a person feels sick or tired, a quick treatment can be used, focusing on the energy of the chakras.

Begin with centreing to the heart.

During this treatment there will be no physical contact between you and the recipient. Usually the person stands up and the therapist stays near the person without touching him.

Sweep the aura with your hands three times.

Concentrate on the positions of the chakras.

Start by placing your hands on the crown chakra, pause there for few minutes, then slowly move your hands on the forehead front and back, pause and move forward on the throat resting there for few minutes and work your way down.

- Place one hand on the heart and the other on the back.
- Place one hand on the solar plexus and the other on the back.
- Place one hand on the sacral chakra and the other on the back.
- Place one hand on the root and the other on the back.
- Finally, sweep the aura from the head to the feet, then shake your hands and conclude the treatment by saying 'Reiki off, reiki off, reiki off'.
- Then place your hands on your own heart chakra to centre yourself.

CHAPTER 20

REIKI FOR ANIMALS

Reiki helps our pet too.

Animals are incapable of being mean, deceitful, unfaithful and cruel. The relationship they have with humans is authentic and those who enjoy this type of relationship with an animal also know the benefits it brings on an emotional level.

Every sensitive soul knows that the communication between animal and human is true, sincere and authentic. Interacting with the animal world brings us back to a pure dimension that can bring out the best in us. Simply put, our pets give us pure love; they teach us the meaning of unconditional love.

In good times or bad, the animal gives itself entirely. It is generous and at times it is capable of taking on the diseases and ill-health conditions of its human guardians, to help lighten the burdens on its human friend.

Animals response to holistic therapies such as Bach flowers, Aura-soma, Reiki, etc., is greater than for humans, since they have no sense of judgment and their purity of soul is unspoiled.

However, any Reiki treatment, or other natural therapy, must not replace veterinary therapies and diagnoses!

In Reiki treatment, you must always telepathically or energetically ask the animal for its permission before starting, its freedom of choice must be respected.

The animal will demonstrate that it accepts the treatment by approaching us, licking us, sniffing us, wagging its tail or expectantly sitting still and waiting.

Conversely, moving away from us, or giving the impression of wanting to bite or annoy us, is a clear message that the animal does not want to be treated.

A horse, for example, will turn around showing us its back. A cat will move briskly away. A dog will get up and go elsewhere.

When an animal does accept the treatment, they clearly feel the energy flowing within them; they often relax until they fall asleep.

Reiki has no contraindications. The important thing is to follow our purest intent towards them, perceiving what the animal wants to communicate to us.

Reiki is useful to those animals that have suffered mistreatment or abuse, or that have been excessively exploited, or kept closed in cages, kennels and zoos.

These animals lack trust in humans, therefore human contact requires greater attention, sensitivity and delicacy. Once they perceive our loving energy then they will allow us to interact with them.

The treatment can be performed in various ways: by placing the hands directly on the animal's body and its chakras, or at a distance.

If an animal has a wound and is agitated, it is better to intervene at a distance by placing the hands in correspondence with the wound.

The animal itself will decide the duration of the treatment. In fact, when it is satisfied that it has received sufficient Reiki energy, it will get up and leave.

Birds, rodents and fish should be treated at a distance either by placing your hands over them in a dome position or, for fish, placing your hands directly on the aquarium.

Reiki can also be given as a prevention when the animal is well.

Cats are very particular and sensitive animals, esoterically predisposed, in fact it is believed that they are suspended between worlds, in a different dimension.

Anyone who has a cat will surely has observed the strange attitudes and behaviors of the feline. He sleeps and wakes up suddenly, running around the house, making puffs and guttural sounds.

He stiffens, stops to look at a wall with his eyes fixed; while we see nothing, they have a very developed openness to subtle energies. They see, feel and perceive situations and vibrations unknown to us.

Therefore, in treating a cat, we may find ourselves in situations different from those encountered when treating a dog.

Each time, we conclude the treatment with loving caresses and sweet words.

At the end of each Reiki treatment, we must thank the universe for allowing us to be a channel and for making the energy flow towards all those who needed it.

Reiki is also very useful for helping our animal friends make their transition to the afterlife, it gives relief, calms fear and anxiety.

Like humans, animals also have an etheric system of chakras. In most animals there are seven main chakras and they are positioned along the spine, more or less in the same way as they are along the human spine.

They are developed differently, though, and there is a difference between domestic and wild animals.

For example, the heart chakra and root chakra are more developed in wild animals, this is motivated by their innate survival instinct.

Differences are also found between artificial and pure breeds, between neutered, sterilised and non-sterilised.

As well as the seven main chakras, there are 21 secondary chakras and six minor chakras.

The secondary chakras are points of energy essential for the vitality of the animal, we find them in the ears, on the nose, and in the tail.

Not all chakras in animals are seen in colour. The main chakra is a coloured centre full of energy. The colours of the chakras vary from animal to animal and as a result of its development. For example, dogs

that help the blind and the disabled; who sacrifice themselves for others, so to speak, may have more open chakras than other animals.
Minors and secondaries are perceived as bright light, usually tending to be white.
Only a few animals have their heart chakra, throat chakra and the third eye chakra opened.

ANIMAL INSTINCTS

Animals have much more developed instincts than humans but it's also very different between species. Dolphins, for example, have this instinct much more evolved.

The instinctive communication of the pet comes from the root chakra. For example, when a cat purrs or sharpens its claws, etc., it wants to communicate its state of being. Also in the paws we find important chakras that are very sensitive points for them as the animal uses them to find harmonious points of energy. As soon as they find such a harmonious energy, they will rub against a tree, on the ground and also against people, so as to stimulate the solar plexus and the root chakra. In doing so, the animal absorbs the energy.

The paw chakras also serve the animal for grounding. Through the chakras of the paws, they feel the vibrations of subtle energies. The change of weather, for example, or if a storm, earthquake or hurricanes are about to happen.

In the tail, an animal has its main and secondary chakras and these also serve to find positive energy. Each chakra corresponds, as in a human being, to a specific organ. Therefore by sending Reiki to a specific chakra, energy will be sent to the corresponding organ.

To rebalance an animal's chakras, you start from the root chakra and, gradually go up, stopping at each energy centre. The treatment will have a shorter duration than that which is practiced on a human being.

The animal will decide when it is time to stop. The duration of treatment will vary each time.

THE REIKI CHAKRAS FOR ANIMALS

FIRST RED CHAKRA

It is located at the base of the tail and affects the glands, spine, bones, hind legs, anus, tail and kidneys.

When the chakra is unbalanced, the animal can show aggression, fears, laziness and restlessness. On the physical level, this manifests as constipation, and weak skeletal and muscular systems.

SECOND CHAKRA ORANGE

It is located above the sexual organs and affects the genitals, pelvis, reproductive organs, intestines, stomach and sacral vertebrae.

When this chakra is unbalanced, the animal will show excessive emotionality. We can see problems with the bladder, or uterus or lower back pain.

It is important to reassure the animal and to educate it with firm but gentle instructions and guidance. Help the animal understand that there is a time for play, for work and for rest.

THIRD YELLOW CHAKRA

This chakra is located on the animal's rib cage and affects the stomach, pancreas, liver, diaphragm, kidneys, nervous system, and lumbar vertebrae.

If unbalanced, it will show up as a lack of willpower, anger, fear, or agitation. Or you may notice the animal has a lot of nervous energy. On the physical level, this manifests as difficult digestion, disordered eating, lack of appetite or nervous hunger. Gently massaging the animal's belly helps a lot.

FOURTH GREEN CHAKRA

It is located in the heart area and affects the heart, circulation, lungs, rib cage and the immune system.

When blocked, the animal can be aggressive and hostile, sad, possessive, jealous. In the physical, this manifests as heart problems. It may help to let the animal have the company of others animals.

FIFTH BLUE CHAKRA

It is located in the upper part of the throat and affects the thyroid gland, the respiratory system, the front legs, the throat, the mouth and the vocal cords.

If unbalanced, the dog could be disobedient, won't listen to commands and is very noisy.

On a physical level, problems with the throat, swallowing, tongue and teeth can occur.

Interact with sweet sounds, softly whisper while talking to the animal.

SIXTH VIOLET CHAKRA

It is located between the eyes and on the head, a little higher above the eyes and affects the head, forehead, ears, nose, nervous system, left eye and the base of the skull.

Its blockage can cause poor concentration, vision problems, frequent ear infections, epilepsy.

SEVENTH WHITE CHAKRA

It is located on the central part of the head, between the ears and affects the skull, the right eye, the cerebral cortex.

When this chakra is unbalanced, it can cause depression and the animal may not want to be touched.

To help the animal find balance and serenity, it may help to sit on the ground and play with the animal, talking softly and playing quiet games.

According to the Reiki principle, each person and each animal can reconnect with their own Universal Energy, of which knowledge has been lost.

This contact for people takes place through 'harmonisation' to Reiki. The Reiki Master reopens our awareness of this source of life and whoever receives it opens his heart again to a feeling of pure Love.

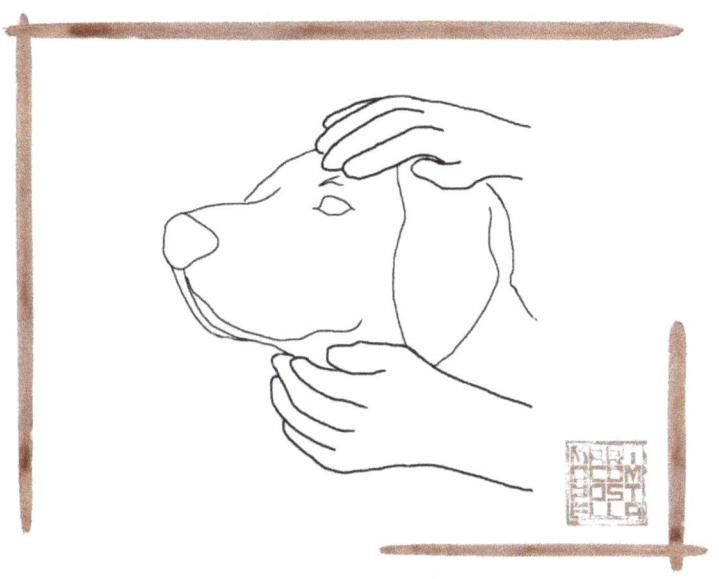

ABOUT THE AUTHOR

GAETANO VIVO

Gaetano Vivo is a Reiki Master who practices in the UK, the US, the Middle East and Italy.

A leading author and speaker on wellness, Gaetano is the author of internationally-acclaimed books and audio books. His website, www.gaetanovivo.com, hosts a one-stop library of resources for optimal wellbeing, including an audiobook and range of CDs.

He is also the founder of the Facebook spiritual channel, *Bridges of Light – Ponti di Luce*, which is a platform for spiritual healers and teachers anywhere to bring their message to the world.

A regular speaker at conferences and workshops around the world, Gaetano also hosts festivals and events, including the International Reiki Festival in Sicily.

He is a member of the Complementary Medical Association of Great Britain, the International Association of Reiki Professionals, and the Noetic Association of America.

LINEAGE OF GAETANO VIVO

Mikao Usui
Chuiro Hayashi
Hawayo Takata
Phyllis Furumoto
William Rand
Gaetano Vivo

The author, Gaetano Vivo, at the tombstone of Reiki founder Mikao Usui in Tokyo. Special permission was granted to visit the site at night.

www.ingramcontent.com/pod-product-compliance
Lightning Source LLC
Chambersburg PA
CBHW041316110526
44591CB00021B/2800